This notebook is intended to be used as part of the ARTES LATINAE program.

ARTES LATINAE   LEVEL TWO

REFERENCE NOTEBOOK

by Waldo E. Sweet

BOLCHAZY-CARDUCCI PUBLISHERS

1000 Brown Street, Wauconda, Illinois 60084

Formerly published by Encyclopaedia Britannica Educational Corporation

CONSULTANTS

Fred W. Householder, Ph.D.
Indiana University

Judith B. Moore
Niles (Michigan) Senior High School

Leonard A. Weinstein
Southfield, Michigan

EDITORS

Barbara H. Rosenwein

Judith N. Levi

Wayne S. Brown

Copyright © 1998 Bolchazy-Carducci Publishers, Inc.

Original Copyright © 1971
by Encyclopaedia Britannica Educational Corporation

All rights reserved.
Printed in the United States of America.

This work may not be transmitted by television or other devices or processed nor copied, recast, transformed, adapted or utilized in any manner, in whole or in part, without a license. For information regarding a license, write:

Bolchazy-Carducci Publishers, Inc.
1000 Brown Street
Wauconda, Illinois 60084
latin@bolchazy.com
http://www.bolchazy.com

1998 Reprint
ISBN 0-86516-303-0

Contents

REFERENCE GRAMMAR, 1

Part I
Morphology, 2
Introduction, 2
Nouns, 2
    Major declensions: 1st, 2d, 3d, 3
    Minor declensions: 4th, 5th, 5
    Comparative table, 6
Adjectives, 6
    Declensions, 7
    Comparison, 8
    Special adjectives, 9
Pronouns, 10
    Personal, 10
    Determinative (**idem**), 12
    Intensifying (**ipse**), 12
    Demonstrative (**hic, ille, iste**), 12
    Relative (**quī**), 13
    Interrogative (**quis**), 13
    Indefinite, 13
Verbs, 14
    Personal endings, 14
    Characteristic vowels, 14
    Principal parts, 15
    Index of conjugations, 16
    Conjugations, 17
    Deponent verbs, 26
    Irregular verbs, 27

Noninflected words, 30
    Coordinating conjunctions, 30
    Subordinating conjunctions, 30
    Sentence connectors, 30
    Interjections, 30
    Intensifiers, 31
    Negators, 31
    Interrogators, 31
    Prepositions, 31
    Qualifiers, 32
    Noun substitutors, 32
    Adverbs, 34
    Adjectivals, 35
Numerals, 35

Part II
Syntax, 39
Introduction, 39
Nouns, 43
    Nominative, 44
    Accusative, 45
    Ablative, 46
    Dative, 50
    Genitive, 52
    Vocative, 53
    Locative, 54
Adjectives, 54
    Function, 54
    Gender, 56

Pronouns, 59
   Personal, 59
   Determinative (**idem**), 60
   Intensifying (**ipse**), 60
   Demonstrative (**hic, ille, iste**), 60
   Relative (**quī**), 61
   Interrogative (**quis**), 62
Verbs, 63
   Person, 63
   Number, 64
   Voice, 64
   Mood, 66
      Indicative, 66
      Imperative, 67
      Subjunctive in main clauses, 67
      Subjunctive in subordinate clauses, 68
      Tense, 71
      Aspect, 75
   Participles, 76
   Verbal nouns, 77
      Infinitive, 77
      Gerund, 79
      Supine, 79
Noninflected words, 79
   Coordinating conjunctions, 79
   Subordinating conjunctions, 80
   Sentence connectors, 81
   Interjections, 82
   Intensifiers, negators, and interrogators, 82
   Prepositions, 83
   Qualifiers, 84
   Noun substitutors, 84
   Adverbs, 84
   Adjectivals, 85

Part III
Selected topics in Latin sentence construction
Word order, 86
Expression of purpose, 89
Indirect discourse, 90
Expression of direct command, 92

Part IV
Advanced notes, 95
  § 1 Regular vowel and consonant changes, 94
  § 2 Locative case, 95
  § 3 Defective nouns, 95
  § 4 Variant nouns of 2d declension, 96
  § 5 Variant nouns of 3d declension, 96
  § 6 Greek noun forms, 96
  § 7 One-, two-, and three- ending 3d declension adjectives
  § 8 Characteristic vowels of verbs, 98
  § 9 Formation of perfective verbs, 99
  § 10 Intransitive verbs, 99
  § 11 Second imperative, 100
  § 12 Noun substitutors, 100
  § 13 Differences between English and Latin number, 100
  § 14 Locative and vocative cases, 101
  § 15 Transitive verbs, 101
  § 16 Dates, 102
  § 17 Word order with ablative, 103
  § 18 Word order with genitive, 103
  § 19 Subjunctive of characteristic, 104
  § 20 Translation of aspect in Latin verbs, 104

BASIC TEXT AND CLOZES, 107
   Introduction, 107
   Basic sentences and readings, 109
   Clozes, 131
      First removal, 131
      Second removal, 152
      Third removal, 173

QUESTION WORDS, 194

INDEX TO SUBJECTS, 199

Reference grammar

This section of the *Reference Notebook* is a summary of the grammar presented in *Artes Latīnae*.[1] It can be used in two ways. It can be either read through for an overview or used to look up individual items, which are listed in the index.

There are three main parts. Part I, Morphology, is a description of the form of Latin words. Part II, Syntax, gives the meaning of these forms in different contexts. Part III, Selected topics in Latin sentence construction, discusses some rules of Latin composition.

ABBREVIATIONS

The following abbreviations and symbols will be used:

* — indicates an imaginary or reconstructed form
∅ — stands for zero letter
§ — Advanced notes (pp. 94-105)
decl — declension
conj — conjugation
m, masc — masculine
f, fem — feminine
n, neut — neuter
nom — nominative
acc — accusative
abl — ablative
dat — dative

gen — genitive
adj(s) — adjective(s)
sg — singular
pl — plural
I — Latin Level I programmed text
II — Latin Level II programmed text
LP — *Lēctiōnēs Primae*
LS — *Lēctiōnēs Secundae*
R — Reading
S — Basic Sentence
BG 1, 2, 3 ... — *Dē Bellō Gallicō*, Book I, of Caesar, chapters 1, 2, 3 ...

A number by itself (1, 2, 3 ...) indicates the Unit number in the Basic Text. Thus for example, I, 2, R3 means Latin Level I, Unit 2, Reading 3. LS4 means *Lēctiōnēs Secundae*, Unit 4.

---

[1] Early Latin, late Latin, and a few structures of classical Latin not included in the course would call for modifications and additions.

Part I
Morphology

INTRODUCTION

Morphology is the study of word forms. In Latin the same word often has different forms, such as **vestis/vestem** or **faciō/faciēbam**. In Latin the noun system (which includes nouns, adjectives, and pronouns) and the verb system make up the class of "inflected" words, words which change form.

There are also words in Latin that do not change form. These are conjunctions (both co-ordinating and subordinating), sentence connectors, interjections, intensifiers, negators, interrogators, prepositions, qualifiers, noun substitutors, adverbs, and adjectivals.

In the following discussion Latin word forms and their patterns of form change are described.[1] The paradigms given are meant to be representative of most words in the same class. Additional, less common paradigms and supplementary material are provided in a section at the back (pp. 94-105) called *Advanced notes.* You will be referred to these *notes* by the symbol §.

NOUNS (for syntax, see pp. 43-54)

Every Latin noun has three distinctive parts. The *stem* carries the lexical meaning. The *characteristic vowel* indicates to which declension the noun belongs, thus allowing us to predict what its form will be in all five cases. The *ending* shows both case and number. Thus in the word **viperam** the stem **viper-** means "snake," the characteristic vowel -a- signals "first declension," and -m signals "accusative singular."

Most Latin nouns have five cases: nominative, accusative, ablative, dative, and genitive. There is also a vocative case, which has the same form as the nominative except for some personal nouns in the second declension masculine.[2] In addition, a few place names have a locative case. See §2 for locative case.

---

[1] See §1 for regular vowel and consonant changes.
[2] See p. 4.

Noun declensions: 1st and 2d

Since most Latin nouns have forms for both singular and plural number, they have a total of ten forms. The small number of Latin nouns with fewer than ten forms are called "defective." See §3 for defective nouns.

The major declensions. The 1st, 2d, and 3d declensions account for 90% of all noun forms in Latin.

First declension

	singular	*plural*
Nom	sīmia∅	sīmiae
Acc	sīmiam	sīmiās
Abl	sīmiā	sīmiīs
Dat	sīmiae	sīmiīs
Gen	sīmiae	sīmiārum

1. Characteristic vowel: -a-
2. Gender: usually feminine

Second declension

sg	pl	sg	pl	sg	pl	sg	pl
lupus	lupī	puer∅	puerī	aper∅	aprī	regnum	regna
lupum	lupōs	puerum	puerōs	aprum	aprōs	rēgnum	rēgna
lupō	lupīs	puerō	puerīs	aprō	aprīs	rēgnō	rēgnīs
lupō	lupīs	puerō	puerīs	aprō	aprīs	rēgnō	rēgnīs
lupī	lupōrum	puerī	puerōrum	aprī	aprōrum	rēgnī	rēgnōrum

1. Characteristic vowel: **-o-** (which disappears before **-ī-**, changes to **-u-** in the sg before final **-s** and final **-m**).
2. Gender: nouns with nom/acc sg ending in **-m**, neut; almost all others, masc., but see p. 58.

3. The nom sg of a few nouns ends in **-r**.[1] The **-e-** before the **-r** is retained in declining some nouns, such as **puer**, gen **puerī**, but dropped in others, such as **aper**, gen **aprī**. Examples from *Artēs Latīnae* include:

-e- before -r retained	-e- before -r dropped
gener, generī	ager, agrī
puer, puerī	aper, aprī
socer, socerī	magister, magistrī

4. The gen sg of nouns whose nom sg endings are **-ius** or **-ium** may be either **-iī** or **-ī** (the form **-ī** is older). Thus the gen sg of **Marius** is **Mariī** or **Marī**.
5. There is a separate vocative form for personal nouns of the 2d decl sg in **-us** and **-ius**: **-e** for nouns ending in **-us** **Mārcus** → **Mārce**; **-ī** for nouns ending in **-ius** **fīlius** → **fīlī**. Exception: the vocative of **deus** is **deus**. The vocative form for all other 2d decl nouns is the same as the nom.
6. See §4 for variant nouns of 2d decl.

Third declension

sg	pl	sg	pl	sg	pl
mīles	mīlitēs	fūr∅	fūrēs	genus∅	genera
mīlitem	mīlitēs	fūrem	fūrēs	genus∅	genera
mīlite	mīlitibus	fūre	fūribus	genere	generibus
mīlitī	mīlitibus	fūrī	fūribus	generī	generibus
mīlitis	mīlitum	fūris	fūrum	generis	generum

sg	pl	sg	pl
fīnis	fīnēs	animal∅	animālia
fīnem	fīnēs, īs	animal∅	animālia
fīne	fīnibus	animālī	animālibus
fīnī	fīnibus	animālī	animālibus
fīnis	fīnium	animālis	animālium

1. Characteristic vowel: **-e-, -i-, ∅**.
2. Gender: may be masc, fem, or neut. See pp. 56-59.
3. Nom sg signal: **-s** or **∅**; all neuts have signal **∅** in the nom/acc sg.

---

[1] This **-r** is in fact the last letter of their stem, so that their characteristic vowel and ending in the nom sg are both **∅**.

Noun declensions: 4th and 5th

4. Subclass of 3d decl nouns (illustrated here by **finis** and **animal**) has gen pl -**ium** and (unless neut) may have acc pl -**is**. Members of this subclass, called **i** stems, include the following:
   a. Most 3d decl nouns with two syllables in both nom and gen, like **finis**.[1]
   b. Most nouns with a stem ending in two consonants, like **mōns, montis**.[2]
   c. Neuters in -**e** (like **mare**), -**al** (like **animal**), and -**ar** (like **exemplar**).
5. See § 5 for variant nouns of 3d decl.

Minor declensions. The 4th and 5th decls each account for about 5% of all noun forms.

Fourth declension

sg	pl	sg	pl
gradus	gradūs	cornū∅[3]	cornua
gradum	gradūs	cornū∅	cornua
gradū	gradibus	cornū∅	cornibus
graduī	gradibus	cornū∅	cornibus
gradūs	graduum	cornūs	cornuum

1. Characteristic vowel: -**u**- (with variant -**i**- in abl and dat pl).
2. Gender of **gradus** type: usually masc (exceptions are **manus, porticus, domus**, and **anus**, which are fem).
3. Gender of **cornū** type: neut[3]

Fifth declension

sg	pl	sg	pl
rēs	rēs	diēs	diēs
rem	rēs	diem	diēs
rē	rēbus	diē	diēbus
reī	rēbus	diēī[4]	diēbus
reī	rērum	diēī[4]	diērum

1. Characteristic vowel: -**ē**-.
2. Gender: always fem except **diēs** (sometimes masc) and **merīdiēs** (always masc).
3. **Rēs** and **diēs** are the only nouns of the 5th decl having all pl forms.

---

[1] But note exceptions such as **canis** (gen pl: **canum**).
[2] But note exceptions such as **māter, mātris** (gen pl: **mātrum**).
[3] Nouns of this type are rare.
[4] The long -**ē**- in forms such as **diēī** is an exception to the rule (see § 1) that a vowel preceding another vowel is always short. This exceptional -**ē**- always appears in the dat and gen sg forms of 5th decl nouns whose nom sg ends in -**iēs**, such as **diēs** and **effigiēs**.

Comparative table of all five declensions

I nom in ∅	II nom in -s	II nom in ∅	II neut	III nom in ∅	III i - stem	III neut	IV	V
Singular								
sīmia	lupus	aper	rēgnum	fūr	fīnis	genus	gradus	rēs
sīmiam	lupum	aprum	rēgnum	fūrem	fīnem	genus	gradum	rem
sīmiā	lupō	aprō	rēgnō	fūre	fīne	genere	gradū	rē
sīmiae	lupō	aprō	rēgnō	fūrī	fīnī	generī	graduī	reī
sīmiae	lupī	aprī	rēgnī	fūris	fīnis	generis	gradūs	reī
Plural								
sīmiae	lupī	aprī	rēgna	fūrēs	fīnēs	genera	gradūs	rēs
sīmiās	lupōs	aprōs	rēgna	fūrēs	fīnēs, īs	genera	gradūs	rēs
sīmiīs	lupīs	aprīs	rēgnīs	fūribus	fīnibus	generibus	gradibus	rēbus
sīmiīs	lupīs	aprīs	rēgnīs	fūribus	fīnibus	generibus	gradibus	rēbus
sīmiārum	lupōrum	aprōrum	rēgnōrum	fūrum	fīnium	generum	graduum	rērum

See § 6 for Greek noun forms.

ADJECTIVES (for syntax, see pp. 54-59)

Adjectives, like nouns, have number and case. Unlike nouns, they are also declined for gender. Thus, for example, the masculine form of the adjective **bonus** will pattern with only certain nouns:

    bonus vir   not   *****bonus puella**

The feminine and neuter forms of the adjective likewise go with only certain nouns. Often the declension of the noun determines the gender of adjective it takes: 1st and 5th declension nouns generally take feminine adjectives, 2d declension nouns generally take masculine or neuter adjectives, and 4th declension nouns generally take masculine adjectives. The gender of adjectives modifying personal nouns, however, regularly reflects the person's sex rather than the noun's declension:[1]

    bona anus   not   *****bonus anus**

---

[1] See Syntax, pp. 56-59.

Adjective declensions: 1st, 2d, and 3d

First and second declension

Singular			*Plural*		
masculine	*feminine*	*neuter*	*masculine*	*feminine*	*neuter*
bonus	bona	bonum	bonī	bonae	bona
bonum	bonam	bonum	bonōs	bonās	bona
bonō	bonā	bonō	bonīs	bonīs	bonīs
bonō	bonae	bonō	bonīs	bonīs	bonīs
bonī	bonae	bonī	bonōrum	bonārum	bonōrum

A few adjs end in **-er** in the masc nom sg. Some of these, such as **līber, lībera, līberum**, retain the **-e-** in their other forms, while others, such as **pulcher, pulchra, pulchrum**, drop the **-e-**.

Third declension

Singular		*Plural*	
m&f	*n*	*m&f*	*n*
facilis	facile∅	facilēs	facilia
facilem	facile∅	facilēs, īs	facilia
facilī	facilī	facilibus	facilibus
facilī	facilī	facilibus	facilibus
facilis	facilis	facilium	facilium

1. Characteristic vowel: -e-, -i-, ∅
2. Most 3d decl adjs have two forms throughout their paradigm: one form for both masc and fem and one form for neut. A few 3d decl adjs, such as **ācer, ācris, ācre**, have three forms in the nom sg, while others, such as **fēlīx**, have only one form in the nom sg. See § 7 for paradigms of 1, 2, and 3 ending adjs.
3. A subclass of 3d decl adjs (usually present participles, such as **vocāns**) has abl sg ending in **-e** (as well as **-ī**), gen pl in **-um** (as well as **-ium**).

Present participle

Singular		Plural	
m&f	*n*	*m&f*	*n*
vocāns	vocāns	vocantēs	vocantia
vocantem	vocāns	vocantēs, -īs	vocantia
vocante, -ī	vocante, -ī	vocantibus	vocantibus
vocantī	vocantī	vocantibus	vocantibus
vocantis	vocantis	vocantium, -um[1]	vocantium, -um[1]

Comparison of adjectives: regular

positive	*comparative*	*superlative*
clārus-a-um, *clear*	clārior, clārius, *clearer*	clārissimus-a-um, *clearest*
fortis-e, *brave*	fortior, fortius, *braver*	fortissimus-a-um, *bravest*
pulcher-chra-chrum, *pretty*	pulchrior, pulchrius, *prettier*	pulcherrimus-a-um, *prettiest*
facilis-e, *easy*	facilior, facilius, *easier*	facillimus-a-um, *easiest*

1. No matter what decl the positive form of the adj is, the comparative is always 3d decl (see p. 9) and the superlative is always 1st or 2d decl.
2. Adjs such as **pulcher**, which end in **-er** (in masc nom sg), form their superlatives by doubling the **-r** and adding **-imus-a-um**.
3. Five common adjs whose stems end in **-il-** form their superlatives by doubling the **-l-** before adding **-imus-a-um**. They are **facilis, difficilis, similis, dissimilis**, and **humilis**. All other adjs in **-il-** (such as **nōbilis**) have regular superlatives, such as **nōbilissimus**.
4. Long adjs often form the comparative with **magis**, *more* and the superlative with **maximē**, *most*, such as **magis formōsa** and **maxime formōsa**.

Comparison of adjectives: irregular

bonus-a-um, *good*	melior, melius, *better*	optimus-a-um, *best*
malus-a-um, *bad*	pejor, pejus, *worse*	pessimus-a-um, *worst*
parvus-a-um, *little*	minor, minus, *less*	minimus-a-um, *least*
magnus-a-um, *great*	major, majus, *greater*	maximus-a-um, *greatest*
multus-a-um, *much*	plūs,[2] *more*	plūrimus-a-um, *most*
multī-ae-a, *many*	plūrēs, plūra,[3] *more*	plūrimī-ae-a, *most*

---

[1] The form **-um** for the gen pl is common in poetry.
[2] There is no comparative adj for **multus**. The neut noun **plūs** is used in its place.
[3] The decl of **plūrēs, plūra** is irregular in that its gen is **plūrium** instead of *****plūrum**.

Adjective declensions: comparatives and special adjectives

Declension of comparatives

Singular		*Plural*	
m&f	n	m&f	n
melior	melius	meliōrēs	meliōra
meliōrem	melius	meliōrēs	meliōra
meliōre, -ī	meliōre, -ī	meliōribus	meliōribus
meliōrī	meliōrī	meliōribus	meliōribus
meliōris	meliōris	meliōrum	meliōrum

Comparative adjs are declined like other 3d decl adjs, with these minor variations:
a. Abl sg ends in **-e**, (rarely in **-ī**).
b. Gen pl ends in **-um**, (instead of **ium**).
c. Characteristic vowel of neut nom/acc pl: ∅ instead of **-i-**. (thus **meliōra** lacks the **-i-** of **facilia**).

Special adjectives[1]

Singular

m	f	n
tōtus	tōta	tōtum
tōtum	tōtam	tōtum
tōtō	tōtā	tōtō
tōtī	tōtī	tōtī
tōtīus[2]	tōtīus[2]	tōtīus[2]

These adjs are 1st and 2d decl variants in the sg. They are completely regular in the pl. In the sg they differ from regular 1st and 2d decl adjs in these two forms:

a. Dat sg ends in **-ī**.
b. Gen sg ends in **-ius**.

---

[1] Many special adjs may be used as pronouns, particularly **alter, alius, neuter, nūllus, ūllus, uter,** and **uterque**.
[2] The variant **-ius** (note short **-i-**) is common in poetry for all special adjs except **alius, alia, aliud**.

c. Other adjs in this class are:

alius, alia, aliud,[1] *other, another*
alter, altera, alterum, *one* (of two), *the other one*
neuter, neutra, neutrum, *neither*
nūllus, nūlla, nūllum, *none, no*
sōlus, sōla, sōlum, *alone, the only*
ūllus, ūlla, ūllum, *any* (in questions, negations, conditions)
ūnus, ūna, ūnum, *one*
uter, utra, utrum, *which?* (of two)
uterque, utraque, utrumque, *each of two, both*

PRONOUNS (for syntax, see pp. 59-63)

Personal pronouns

The personal pronouns of the 1st and 2d persons have a unique declension. Those used for the 3d person (**is, ea, id**) are declined like special adjectives (**tōtus, alter,** etc.), and therefore have the distinctive forms **-i** in the dative singular and **-ius** (or **-jus**) in the genitive singular. They may be used as adjectives as well as pronouns. Other pronouns, such as **hic** and **ille,** may also be used for the 3d person, but these have demonstrative force.

1st person		2d person	
sg	pl	sg	pl
egō	nōs	tū	vōs
mē	nōs	tē	vōs
mē	nōbīs	tē	vōbīs
mihī, mī[2]	nōbīs	tibī[2]	vōbīs
meī[3]	nostrum, ī[3]	tuī[3]	vestrum, ī[3]

---

[1] Note the neuter in **-d.**
[2] The forms **mihi** and **tibi** (with the final vowel short) are common.
[3] These gen forms rarely occur. Instead, the adjs **meus, tuus, noster,** and **vester** are used to show possession.

Pronouns: 3d person

3d person

sg			pl		
is	ea	id	eī, ī	eae	ea
eum	eam	id	eōs	eās	ea
eō	eā	eō	eīs, īs	eīs, īs	eīs, īs
eī	eī	eī	eīs, īs	eīs, īs	eīs, īs
ejus	ejus	ejus	eōrum	eārum	eōrum

The reflexive forms[1] for the 1st and 2d personal pronouns are the same as those for non-reflexive uses. Thus mē may be used in both of the following sentences:

> **Mē** spectō. *I am watching myself.*
> **Mē** spectat. *He is watching me.*

However, the reflexive forms for the 3d person are distinct:

> **Eum** spectō. *I am watching him.*
> **Sē** spectat. *He is watching himself.*

3d person reflexive

sg & pl
—
sē, sēsē
sē, sēsē
sibī[2]
suī

Other pronouns

These are declined like is and may be used as adjectives as well as pronouns. For syntax see pp. 59-63.

---

[1] For the definition and use of the reflexive, see Syntax, p. 59.
[2] Sĭbĭ (note short -i) is also common.

Determinative pronoun and adjective: īdem

sg			pl		
īdem	eadem	idem	eīdem, īdem	eaedem	eadem
eundem	eandem	idem	eōsdem	eāsdem	eadem
eōdem	eādem	eōdem	eīsdem, īsdem	eīsdem, īsdem	eīsdem, īsdem
eīdem	eīdem	eīdem	eīsdem, īsdem	eīsdem, īsdem	eīsdem, īsdem
ejusdem	ejusdem	ejusdem	eōrundem	eārundem	eōrundem

Intensifying pronoun and adjective: ipse

sg			pl		
ipse	ipsa	ipsum	ipsī	ipsae	ipsa
ipsum	ipsam	ipsum	ipsōs	ipsās	ipsa
ipsō	ipsā	ipsō	ipsīs	ipsīs	ipsīs
ipsī	ipsī	ipsī	ipsīs	ipsīs	ipsīs
ipsīus	ipsīus	ipsīus	ipsōrum	ipsārum	ipsōrum

Demonstrative pronouns and adjectives: hic, ille, iste

hic[1]

sg			pl		
hic[2]	haec	hoc[2]	hī	hae	haec
hunc	hanc	hoc	hōs	hās	haec
hōc	hāc	hōc	hīs	hīs	hīs
huic	huic	huic	hīs	hīs	hīs
hujus	hujus	hujus	hōrum	hārum	hōrum

ille

sg			pl		
ille	illa	illud	illī	illae	illa
illum	illam	illud	illōs	illās	illa
illō	illā	illō	illīs	illīs	illīs
illī	illī	illī	illīs	illīs	illīs
illīus	illīus	illīus	illōrum	illārum	illōrum

---

[1] The particle -ce is sometimes added to **hujus, hōs, hās,** and **his**, giving forms like **hujusce**.
[2] The variants **hicc** (commonly) and **hocc** (always) are used when they precede a word beginning with a vowel.

iste

sg			pl		
iste	ista	istud	istī	istae	ista
istum	istam	istud	istōs	istās	ista
istō	istā	istō	istīs	istīs	istīs
istī	istī	istī	istīs	istīs	istīs
istīus	istīus	istīus	istōrum	istārum	istōrum

Relative pronoun and adjective: qui

sg			pl		
quī	quae	quod	quī	quae	quae
quem	quam	quod	quōs	quās	quae
quō	quā	quō	quibus	quibus	quibus
cui	cui	cui	quibus	quibus	quibus
cujus	cujus	cujus	quōrum	quārum	quōrum

Interrogative pronoun and adjective: quis

sg		pl		
m&f	n	m	f	n
quis	quid	quī	quae	quae rēs
quem	quid	quōs	quās	quās rēs
quō	quō	quibus	quibus	quibus
cui	cui	quibus	quibus	quibus
cujus	cujus	quōrum	quārum	quōrum

Indefinite pronouns and adjectives

Indefinite pronouns and adjectives are formed on the relative or interrogative pronoun. The most common are

> **aliquis, aliquid,** *someone, something*[1]
> **quidam, quaedam, quoddam,**[2] *a certain*
> **quicumque, quaecumque, quodcumque,** *whosoever, whatsoever*

---

[1] In **si** clauses, the **ali-** is usually deleted, leaving **si quis** or **si quid**. The pronoun **aliquis** has the adj form **aliquī, aliqua, aliquod**.

[2] Declined like **quī, quae, quod** but with the **-m** changed to **-n**, as in **quendam, quandam, quōrundem,** etc.

quīlibet, quaelibet, quodlibet, *every*
quisquam, quicquam (quidquam), *anybody*
quisque, quaeque, quodque, *each one*
quisquis, quaequae, quodquod,[1] *whosoever, whatsoever*
quīvīs, quaevīs, quodvīs, *anyone at all*

VERBS (for syntax, see pp. 63-75)

Most Latin verb forms may be divided into several parts. Consider the verb form **laudābās**. The lexical stem **laud-** tells the meaning of the verb. The characteristic vowel[2] -ā- shows which conjugation the verb belongs to. The **-bā-** shows the tense (past), the aspect (imperfective), and the mood (indicative). The ending -s shows the person (second), the number (singular), and the voice (active).[3]

Personal endings are as follows:

Active endings for all tenses except #5		Active endings for tense #5		Passive endings for tenses #1, #2, #3, #7, #8[4]	
-ō, -m	-mus	-ī	-imus	-r	-mur
-s	-tis	-istī	-istis	-ris	-minī
-t	-nt, -unt	-it	-ērunt, -ēre	-tur	-ntur, -untur

The characteristic vowels of each conjugation are as follows: (See §8)

1st: -ā- as in **laudāre**
2d: -ē- as in **movēre**
3d: -e- as in **agere** and **capere**
4th: -ī- as in **audīre**

---

[1] **Quidquid** and **quicquid** are variants of **quodquod**. Note that both parts of this word are declined.
[2] See §8 for further discussion of characteristic vowels.
[3] See syntax pp. 63-75 for definitions of person, number, voice, mood, tense, and aspect.
[4] The perfective tenses (#4, #5, #6, #9, and #10) do not have passive personal endings. The passive perfective is expressed instead by the perfective passive participle plus the verb **sum**.

Regular verbs: principal parts

The principal parts of five typical verbs that will be used to illustrate the forms of each conjugation[1] are

1st conj:	laudō, laudāre, laudāvī, laudātus
2d conj:	moveō, movēre, mōvī, mōtus
3d conj:	agō, agere, ēgī, āctus
3d conj-iō:	capiō, capere, cēpī, captus
4th conj:	audiō, audīre, audīvī, audītus

The first principal part, such as **laudō**, is the #2 (present imperfective) form for the 1st person sg active.[2]

The second principal part, such as **laudāre,** is the imperfective active infinitive (also called the present infinitive). The imperfective stem is obtained by dropping the **-re**. All imperfective forms are formed on this stem except the future active participle.

The third principal part, such as **laudāvī**, is the #5 (present perfective) form for the 1st person sg active. The perfective active stem is obtained by dropping the ending **-ī**. All active perfective forms are based on this stem. See § 9 for formation of perfective active stem.

The fourth principal part, such as **laudātus,** is the perfective passive participle. The perfective passive stem is obtained by dropping the **-us** ending. All perfective passive forms, the future active participle, and the supine are based on this stem. See § 10 for verbs that lack the 4th principal part.

---

[1] For the conjugation of irregular verbs, see p. 27.
[2] The only reason for including this principal part is to distinguish the two kinds of 3d conj verbs, that is, verbs such as **agō** and **capiō**.

The following is an overview of the verb system, using **laudat** as a model:

	past	present	future
indicative imperfective	#1 laudābat laudābātur	#2 laudat laudātur	#3 laudābit laudābitur
perfective	#4 laudāverat laudātus erat[1]	#5 laudāvit laudātus est	#6 laudāverit laudātus erit
subjunctive imperfective	#7 laudāret laudārētur	#8 laudet laudētur	
perfective	#9 laudāvisset laudātus esset	#10 laudāverit laudātus sit	
imperative		#11 laudā	

Conjugations of regular verbs

Complete conjugations for all five typical verbs are given below. They are arranged in the following order:

Imperfective

Active   Passive

indicative   *indicative*

#1 Past   p. 17   #1 Past   p. 19
#2 Present   p. 18   #2 Present   p. 19
#3 Future   p. 18   #3 Future   p. 19

---

[1] **Laudātus** is decl for gender and number. Since it refers to the subject, it is always in the nom case.

Regular verbs: index of conjugations

subjunctive *subjunctive*

#7 Past   p. 18   #7 Past   p. 20
#8 Present p. 18   #8 Present p. 20

imperative

#11   p. 19

Perfective

indicative   *indicative*

#4 Past   p. 21   #4 Past   p. 22
#5 Present p. 21   #5 Present p. 23
#6 Future p. 21   #6 Future p. 23

subjunctive   *subjunctive*

#9 Past   p. 22   #9 Past   p. 23
#10 Present p. 22   #10 Present p. 23

Infinitives p. 24
Participles p. 24
Supine   p. 25
Gerunds   p. 25

Imperfective aspect

The imperfective tenses and moods are formed on the imperfective stem, obtained by dropping the **-re** from the imperfective active infinitive.

Active Voice

Indicative mood

1st	2d	3d	3d -iō	4th
#1 Past imperfective indicative				
laudābam	movēbam	agēbam	capiēbam	audiēbam
laudābās	movēbās	agēbās	capiēbās	audiēbās
laudābat	movēbat	agēbat	capiēbat	audiēbat
laudābāmus	movēbāmus	agēbāmus	capiēbāmus	audiēbāmus
laudābātis	movēbātis	agēbātis	capiēbātis	audiēbātis
laudābant	movēbant	agēbant	capiēbant	audiēbant

1st	2d	3d	3d -iō	4th

#2 Present imperfective indicative

1st	2d	3d	3d -iō	4th
laudō	moveō	agō	capiō	audiō
laudās	movēs	agis	capis	audīs
laudat	movet	agit	capit	audit
laudāmus	movēmus	agimus	capimus	audīmus
laudātis	movētis	agitis	capitis	audītis
laudant	movent	agunt	capiunt	audiunt

#3 Future imperfective indicative

1st	2d	3d	3d -iō	4th
laudābō	movēbō	agam	capiam	audiam
laudābis	movēbis	agēs	capiēs	audiēs
laudābit	movēbit	aget	capiet	audiet
laudābimus	movēbimus	agēmus	capiēmus	audiēmus
laudābitis	movēbitis	agētis	capiētis	audiētis
laudābunt	movēbunt	agent	capient	audient

Active voice

Subjunctive mood

1st	2d	3d	3d -iō	4th

#7 Past imperfective subjunctive

1st	2d	3d	3d -iō	4th
laudārem	movērem	agerem	caperem	audīrem
laudārēs	movērēs	agerēs	caperēs	audīrēs
laudāret	movēret	ageret	caperet	audīret
laudārēmus	movērēmus	agerēmus	caperēmus	audīrēmus
laudārētis	movērētis	agerētis	caperētis	audīrētis
laudārent	movērent	agerent	caperent	audīrent

#8 Present imperfective subjunctive

1st	2d	3d	3d -iō	4th
laudem	moveam	agam	capiam	audiam
laudēs	moveās	agās	capiās	audiās
laudet	moveat	agat	capiat	audiat
laudēmus	moveāmus	agāmus	capiāmus	audiāmus
laudētis	moveātis	agātis	capiātis	audiātis
laudent	moveant	agant	capiant	audiant

Regular verb conjugations

Imperative mood

1st	2d	3d	3d -iō	4th

#11 First imperative

| sg: | laudā | movē | age[1] | cape | audī |
| pl: | laudāte | movēte | agite | capite | audīte |

See §11 for the Second Imperative

Passive voice

Indicative mood

1st	2d	3d	3d -iō	4th

#1 Past imperfective indicative

laudābar	movēbar	agēbar	capiēbar	audiēbar
laudābāris[2]	movēbāris[2]	agēbāris[2]	capiēbāris[2]	audiēbāris[2]
laudābātur	movēbātur	agēbātur	capiēbātur	audiēbātur
laudābāmur	movēbāmur	agēbāmur	capiēbāmur	audiēbāmur
laudābāminī	movēbāminī	agēbāminī	capiēbāminī	audiēbāminī
laudābantur	movēbantur	agēbantur	capiēbantur	audiēbantur

#2 Present imperfective indicative

laudor	moveor	agor	capior	audior
laudāris[2]	movēris[2]	ageris[2]	caperis[2]	audīris[2]
laudātur	movētur	agitur	capitur	audītur
laudāmur	movēmur	agimur	capimur	audīmur
laudāminī	movēminī	agiminī	capiminī	audīminī
laudantur	moventur	aguntur	capiuntur	audiuntur

#3 Future imperfective indicative

laudābor	movēbor	agar	capiar	audiar
laudāberis[2]	movēberis[2]	agēris[2]	capiēris[2]	audiēris[2]
laudābitur	movēbitur	agētur	capiētur	audiētur
laudābimur	movēbimur	agēmur	capiēmur	audiēmur
laudābiminī	movēbiminī	agēminī	capiēminī	audiēminī
laudābuntur	movēbuntur	agentur	capientur	audientur

---

[1] But note the irregular forms **dīc, dūc, fac, fer,** which lack the final **-e.**

[2] A variant of **-ris** is **-re.**

Passive voice

Subjunctive mood

1st	2d	3d	3d -iō	4th

#7 Past imperfective subjunctive

1st	2d	3d	3d -iō	4th
laudārer	movērer	agerer	caperer	audīrer
laudārēris[1]	movērēris[1]	agerēris[1]	caperēris[1]	audīrēris[1]
laudārētur	movērētur	agerētur	caperētur	audīrētur
laudārēmur	movērēmur	agerēmur	caperēmur	audīrēmur
laudārēminī	movērēminī	agerēminī	caperēminī	audīrēminī
laudārentur	movērentur	agerentur	caperentur	audīrentur

#8 Present imperfective subjunctive

1st	2d	3d	3d -iō	4th
lauder	movear	agar	capiar	audiar
laudēris[1]	moveāris[1]	agāris[1]	capiāris[1]	audiāris[1]
laudētur	moveātur	agātur	capiātur	audiātur
laudēmur	moveāmur	agāmur	capiāmur	audiāmur
laudēminī	moveāminī	agāminī	capiāminī	audiāminī
laudentur	moveantur	agantur	capiantur	audiantur

Future passive participle (gerundive)

1st	2d	3d	3d -iō	4th
laudandus	movendus	agendus	capiendus	audiendus

---

[1] A variant of -ris is -re.

Regular verb conjugations

Perfective aspect

Active voice

The active forms of the perfective aspect are formed on the perfective active stem, obtained by dropping the -ī of the third principal part.

Indicative mood

1st	2d	3d	3d -iō	4th
#4 Past perfective indicative				
laudāveram[1]	mōveram	ēgeram	cēperam	audīveram[1]
laudāverās	mōverās	ēgerās	cēperās	audīverās
laudāverat	mōverat	ēgerat	cēperat	audīverat
laudāverāmus	mōverāmus	ēgerāmus	cēperāmus	audīverāmus
laudāverātis	mōverātis	ēgerātis	cēperātis	audīverātis
laudāverant	mōverant	ēgerant	ceperant	audīverant
#5 Present perfective indicative				
laudāvī	mōvī	ēgī	cēpī	audīvī
laudāvistī	mōvistī	ēgistī	cēpistī	audīvistī
laudāvit	mōvit	ēgit	cēpit	audīvit
laudāvimus	mōvimus	ēgimus	cēpimus	audīvimus
laudāvistis	mōvistis	ēgistis	cēpistis	audīvistis
laudāvērunt[2]	mōvērunt[2]	ēgērunt[2]	cēpērunt[2]	audīvērunt[2]
#6 Future perfective indicative				
laudāverō	mōverō	ēgerō	cēperō	audīverō
laudāveris[3]	mōveris[3]	ēgeris[3]	cēperis[3]	audīveris[3]
laudāverit	mōverit	ēgerit	cēperit	audīverit
laudāverimus	mōverimus	ēgerimus	cēperimus	audīverimus
laudāveritis	mōveritis	ēgeritis	cēperitis	audīveritis
laudāverint	mōverint	ēgerint	cēperint	audīverint

---

[1] Contracted forms (indicated in *Artēs Latīnae* by an apostrophe) are common in all moods and tenses of the active perfective system for verbs whose perfective active stem ends in -v- preceded by a vowel, such as **laudāveram** → **laudā'ram**; **audīvistis** → **audī'stis**; **dēlēvisse** → **dēlē'sse**. However, not all forms have a contracted variant.

[2] These 3d person pl forms have the following common variants: **laudāvēre, mōvēre, ēgēre, cēpēre, audīvēre,** as well as contracted forms, such as **laudā'runt** and **audī'runt**.

[3] A variant of **-ris** is **-re**.

Subjunctive mood

1st	2d	3d	3d -iō	4th

#9 Past perfective subjunctive

1st	2d	3d	3d -iō	4th
laudāvissem	mōvissem	ēgissem	cēpissem	audīvissem
laudāvissēs	mōvissēs	ēgissēs	cēpissēs	audīvissēs
laudāvisset	mōvisset	ēgisset	cēpisset	audīvisset
laudāvissēmus	mōvissēmus	ēgissēmus	cēpissēmus	audīvissēmus
laudāvissētis	mōvissētis	ēgissētis	cēpissētis	audīvissētis
laudāvissent	mōvissent	ēgissent	cēpissent	audīvissent

#10 Present perfective subjunctive

1st	2d	3d	3d -iō	4th
laudāverim	mōverim	ēgerim	cēperim	audīverim
laudāverīs[1]	mōverīs[1]	ēgerīs[1]	cēperīs[1]	audīverīs[1]
laudāverit	mōverit	ēgerit	cēperit	audīverit
laudāverīmus	mōverīmus	ēgerīmus	cēperīmus	audīverīmus
laudāverītis[1]	mōverītis[1]	ēgerītis[1]	cēperītis[1]	audīverītis[1]
laudāverint	mōverint	ēgerint	cēperint	audīverint

Passive voice

Latin does not have inflected verb forms with passive personal endings to express the *perfective* passive. Instead, the perfective passive participle is used with a form of the verb **sum**.[2] The participle agrees with the subject in number, gender, and case (which is always nominative).

Indicative mood

1st	2d	3d	3d -iō	4th

#4 Past perfective indicative

1st	2d	3d	3d -iō	4th
laudātus eram	mōtus eram	āctus eram	captus eram	audītus eram
laudātus erās	mōtus erās	āctus erās	captus erās	audītus erās
laudātus erat	mōtus erat	āctus erat	captus erat	audītus erat
laudātī erāmus	mōtī erāmus	āctī erāmus	captī erāmus	audītī erāmus
laudātī erātis	mōtī erātis	āctī erātis	captī erātis	audītī erātis
laudātī erant	mōtī erant	āctī erant	captī erant	audītī erant

---

[1] A common variant is **-eri-** (note short i).
[2] When easily understood, the verb **sum** is often omitted.

Regular verb conjugations

1st	2d	3d	3d -iō	4th

#5 Present perfective indicative

1st	2d	3d	3d -iō	4th
laudātus sum	mōtus sum	āctus sum	captus sum	audītus sum
laudātus es	mōtus es	āctus es	captus es	audītus es
laudātus est	mōtus est	āctus est	captus est	audītus est
laudātī sumus	mōtī sumus	āctī sumus	captī sumus	audītī sumus
laudātī estis	mōtī estis	āctī estis	captī estis	audītī estis
laudātī sunt	mōtī sunt	āctī sunt	captī sunt	audītī sunt

#6 Future perfective indicative

1st	2d	3d	3d -iō	4th
laudātus erō	mōtus erō	āctus erō	captus erō	audītus erō
laudātus eris	mōtus eris	āctus eris	captus eris	audītus eris
laudātus erit	mōtus erit	āctus erit	captus erit	audītus erit
laudātī erimus	mōtī erimus	āctī erimus	captī erimus	audītī erimus
laudātī eritis	mōtī eritis	āctī eritis	captī eritis	audītī eritis
laudātī erunt	mōtī erunt	āctī erunt	captī erunt	audītī erunt

Subjunctive mood

1st	2d	3d	3d -iō	4th

#9 Past perfective subjunctive

1st	2d	3d	3d -iō	4th
laudātus essem	mōtus essem	āctus essem	captus essem	audītus essem
laudātus essēs	mōtus essēs	āctus essēs	captus essēs	audītus essēs
laudātus esset	mōtus esset	āctus esset	captus esset	audītus esset
laudātī essēmus	mōtī essēmus	āctī essēmus	captī essēmus	audītī essēmus
laudātī essētis	mōtī essētis	āctī essētis	captī essētis	audītī essētis
laudātī essent	mōtī essent	āctī essent	captī essent	audītī essent

#10 Present perfective subjunctive

1st	2d	3d	3d -iō	4th
laudātus sim	mōtus sim	āctus sim	captus sim	audītus sim
laudātus sīs	mōtus sīs	āctus sīs	captus sīs	audītus sīs
laudātus sit	mōtus sit	āctus sit	captus sit	audītus sit
laudātī sīmus	mōtī sīmus	āctī sīmus	captī sīmus	audītī sīmus
laudātī sītis	mōtī sītis	āctī sītis	captī sītis	audītī sītis
laudātī sint	mōtī sint	āctī sint	captī sint	audītī sint

Infinitives

1st	2d	3d	3d -iō	4th
Imperfective active infinitive				
laudāre	movēre	agere	capere	audīre
Imperfective passive infinitive				
laudārī	movērī	agī	capī	audīrī
Perfective active infinitive				
laudāvisse	mōvisse	ēgisse	cēpisse	audīvisse
Perfective passive infinitive				
laudātus esse	mōtus esse	āctus esse	captus esse	audītus esse
Future active infinitive				
laudātūrus esse	mōtūrus esse	āctūrus esse	captūrus esse	audītūrus esse
Future passive infinitive[1]				
laudātus īrī	mōtus īrī	āctus īrī	captus īrī	audītus īrī

Participles

1st	2d	3d	3d -iō	4th
Imperfective active ("present") participle				
laudāns	movēns	agēns	capiēns	audiēns
Perfective passive ("past") participle				
laudātus	mōtus	āctus	captus	audītus
Future active participle[2]				
laudātūrus	mōtūrus	āctūrus	captūrus	audītūrus

---

[1] This infinitive is extremely rare.
[2] Note that this future *imperfective active* participle is constructed on a stem obtained from the *perfective passive* participle.

Regular verb conjugations

1st	2d	3d	3d -iō	4th

Future passive participle (gerundive)

laudandus	movendus	agendus	capiendus	audiendus

Supine

The supine is formed on the stem of the perfective passive participle.

	1st	2d	3d	3d -iō	4th
acc:	laudātum	mōtum	āctum	captum	audītum
abl:	laudātū	mōtū	āctū	captū	audītū

Gerunds

	1st	2d	3d	3d -iō	4th
acc:	laudandum	movendum	agendum	capiendum	audiendum
abl:	laudandō	movendō	agendō	capiendō	audiendō
dat:	laudandō	movendō	agendō	capiendō	audiendō
gen:	laudandī	movendī	agendī	capiendī	audiendī

Conjugations of deponent verbs

Deponent verbs have passive endings but are active in meaning.[1] The paradigm of a deponent verb of any conjugation is like the passive of a regular transitive verb of that conjugation.[2]

In terms of the paradigms we have used, the conjugation of deponents may be systematized as follows:

Paradigm of		Paradigm[3] of
1st conj passive **laudor-ārī-ātus sum**	=	1st conj deponent **mīror-ārī-ātus sum**
2d conj passive **moveor, movērī, mōtus sum**	=	2d conj deponent **vereor, verērī, veritus sum**
3d conj passive **agor, agī, āctus sum**	=	3d conj deponent **loquor, loquī, locūtus sum**
3d -iō conj passive **capior, capī, captus sum**	=	3d -iō conj deponent **morior, morī, mortuus sum**
4th conj passive **audior-īrī-ītus sum**	=	4th conj deponent **mentior-īrī-ītus sum**

---

[1] An exception is the gerundive, which always has a passive meaning regardless of the verb on which it is formed: **mīrandus** means *should be admired*.

[2] The one form that is an apparent exception is the singular imperative of deponents, which has the ending -re, such as **moderāre!** *be moderate!;* **ūtere!** *use!* **verēre!** *fear!* However, the forms are in fact identical to the extremely rare passive imperative, **laudāre!** *be praised!*

[3] The imperfective stem of a deponent verb is obtained by removing the -rī from the second principal part (except for 3d conj deponents, where the -ī is simply changed to -e-.)

Conjugations of irregular verbs[1]

Only a few Latin verbs do not fit into the patterns of the four regular conjugations.

Principal parts:

sum, esse,[2] fui, futūrus[3]	nōlō, nōlle, nōluī
possum, posse, potuī	mālō, mālle, māluī[4]
ferō, ferre, tulī, lātus	eō, īre, iī,[5] itūrus[6]
volō, velle, voluī	fīō,[7] fierī (and fierī), factus sum

• Most of the irregularities of these verbs occur in the #2 tense (present imperfective indicative). Sum and its compound possum, however, are irregular in all tenses of the imperfective system.

• Volō and its compounds nōlō and mālō are irregular in the #8 tense (present imperfective subjunctive) as well as in the #2 tense.

• Ferō is the only one of these irregular verbs with passive forms.[8]

• Since all irregular verbs have regular perfective forms, only the imperfective system will be given here.

Imperfective aspect

Active voice

Indicative mood

#1 Past imperfective indicative

eram	poteram	ferēbam	volēbam	nōlēbam	mālēbam	ībam	fīēbam
erās	poterās	ferēbās	volēbās	nōlēbās	mālēbās	ībās	fīēbās
erat	poterat	ferēbat	volēbat	nōlēbat	mālēbat	ībat	fīēbat
erāmus	poterāmus	ferēbāmus	volēbāmus	nōlēbāmus	mālēbāmus	ībāmus	fīēbāmus
erātis	poterātis	ferēbātis	volēbātis	nōlēbātis	mālēbātis	ībātis	fīēbātis
erant	poterant	ferēbant	volēbant	nōlēbant	mālēbant	ībant	fīēbant

---

[1] The 3d conj verb edere might be added to this list, because in addition to its regular forms, it has the irregular #2 forms ēs, ēst, and ēstis and the imperfective infinitive ēsse.

[2] Sum has a special infinitive, fore, which indicates future time.

[3] This is the future active participle. It is sometimes given as the 4th principal part of a verb that lacks a perfective passive participle.

[4] Mālō is a compound of magis and volō and means *to prefer*.

[5] The variant form īvī is rare.

[6] This is the future active participle.

[7] Fīō is unusual throughout its paradigm because the -i- is not shortened before another vowel. See § 1 for vowel shortening.

[8] However, compounds of eō that take direct objects, such as transeō, also have passive forms.

Active voice

#2 Present imperfective indicative

sum	possum	ferō	volō	nōlō	mālō	eō	fīō
es	potes	fers	vīs	nōn vīs	māvīs	īs	fīs
est	potest	fert	vult	nōn vult	māvult	it	fit
sumus	possumus	ferimus	volumus	nōlumus	mālumus	īmus	fīmus
estis	potestis	fertis	vultis	nōn vultis	māvultis	ītis	fītis
sunt	possunt	ferunt	volunt	nōlunt	mālunt	eunt	fīunt

#3 Future imperfective indicative

erō	poterō	feram	volam	nōlam	mālam	ībō	fīam
eris	poteris	ferēs	volēs	nōlēs	mālēs	ībis	fīēs
erit	poterit	feret	volet	nōlet	mālet	ībit	fīet
erimus	poterimus	ferēmus	volēmus	nōlēmus	mālēmus	ībimus	fīēmus
eritis	poteritis	ferētis	volētis	nōlētis	mālētis	ībitis	fīētis
erunt	poterunt	ferent	volent	nōlent	mālent	ībunt	fīent

Subjunctive mood

#7 Past imperfective subjunctive

essem[1]	possem	ferrem	vellem	nōllem	māllem	īrem	fierem
essēs	possēs	ferrēs	vellēs	nōllēs	māllēs	īrēs	fierēs
esset	posset	ferret	vellet	nōllet	māllet	īret	fieret
essēmus	possēmus	ferrēmus	vellēmus	nōllēmus	māllēmus	īrēmus	fierēmus
essētis	possētis	ferrētis	vellētis	nōllētis	māllētis	īrētis	fierētis
essent	possent	ferrent	vellent	nōllent	māllent	īrent	fierent

#8 Present imperfective subjunctive

sim	possim	feram	velim	nōlim	mālim	eam	fīam
sīs	possīs	ferās	velīs	nōlīs	mālīs	eās	fīās
sit	possit	ferat	velit	nōlit	mālit	eat	fīat
sīmus	possīmus	ferāmus	velīmus	nōlīmus	mālīmus	eāmus	fīāmus
sītis	possītis	ferātis	velītis	nōlītis	mālītis	eātis	fīātis
sint	possint	ferant	velint	nōlint	mālint	eant	fīant

---

[1] The forms **forem, forēs,** etc. are variants of **essem, essēs,** etc.

Irregular verb conjugations

Present active participle

——— ——— ferēns volēns nōlēns ——— iēns ———
                                          (gen, euntis)

Future active participle

futūrus ——— lātūrus ——— ——— ——— itūrus faciendus

Passive voice

The only one of these irregular verbs with forms in the passive voice is **ferō**. Of these forms, only the forms for the present imperfective (#2) are irregularly formed; the other forms are like those of a regular 3d conj verb.

Indicative mood

#1 Past imperfective

ferēbar etc.

#2 Present imperfective

feror	ferimur
ferris	feriminī
fertur	feruntur

#3 Future imperfective

ferar etc.

Subjunctive mood

#7 Past imperfective

ferrer etc.

#8 Present imperfective

ferar etc.

Perfective aspect

As noted above, the perfective system of irregular verbs is regularly formed.[1]

---

[1] **Eō** is an exception. Some of its #5 forms may be contracted, giving, for example, **īt** instead of **iit**.

NONINFLECTED WORDS

Noninflected words do not change form. In Latin these are comparatively few in number but high in frequency. The following occur in *Artēs Latīnae:*

1. **Coordinating conjunctions** (for syntax see p. 79)

ac/atque	-que
aut	sed
et	sīve/seu
nec/neque	vel/ve

2. **Subordinating conjunctions** (for syntax, see p. 80)

cum	nī/nisī	quia	tamquam
dōnec	postquam	quīn	ut
dum	priusquam	seu/sīve	velut
licet	quamquam	sī	
nē	quamvīs	sīcut	
neu/nēve	quasī	simul (simul atque, simul ac)	

3. **Sentence connectors** (for syntax, see p. 81)

at	enim	nam	tandem
autem	ergō	namque	vērō
deinde/dein	igitur	quīn	vērum
dēmum	immō	quod sī	
dēnique	itaque	sīn	

4. **Interjections** (for syntax, see p. 82)

ecce!	heu!
ei!	heus!
ēn!	meherculēs (meherculē!)
hercle!	Ō!

5a. Intensifiers (for syntax, see p. 82)

equidem[1]	modo	quidem
et	nē[2]	quoque
etiam	nempe	scīlicet
forsan	nōn ... sōlum	tamen
forsitan	praesertim	ūsque
fortasse	procul	ut/utinam[3]
ita	profectō	valdē
jam	quamquam	vel

5b. Negators (for syntax see p. 82)

haud	nōn
nē	nōndum
nē ... quidem	scīlicet

5c. Interrogators (for syntax see p. 82)

an	nōnne	utrum
-ne	num	

6. Prepositions (for syntax, see p. 83)

a. Which pattern with the acc

ad	citrā	intrā	prope
adversus/adversum	contrā	juxtā	propter
ante	extrā	ob	sub
apud	in	per	suprā
circā	infrā	post	trāns
circum	inter	praeter	ultrā

b. Which pattern with the abl

ā/ab	palam
cōram	prae
cum	prō
dē	sine
ē/ex	sub
in	

---

[1] Usually found only with a verb in the 1st person.
[2] Used with the subjunctive to indicate negative wish.
[3] Used with the subjunctive to indicate wish.

c. *Which pattern with either acc or abl*

in
sub

7. Qualifiers (for syntax, see p. 84)

ad	male	parum	sat/satis
adeō	maximē	prope	tam
aegrē	nēquāquam	quam	vix
bene	nimis	quamlibet	
circiter[1]	omnīnō	quamvīs	
magis	paene	quasī	

8. Noun substitutors[2]

A noun substitutor is a single word used in place of a noun phrase. **Ubi,** for example, substitutes for the noun phrase **quō locō**; **hīc** substitutes for the noun phrase **hōc locō**. The noun substitutors used in *Artēs Latīnae* are listed below. Although we have usually given just one equivalent noun phrase to suggest the general meaning, many of these noun substitutors may be used in both spatial and temporal senses (as shown, for example, for **adhūc**) and even in other senses by extension (such as **illō** to mean **ad illam rem**, *to that purpose*).

noun substitutor	*equivalent noun phrase*
ab	ab hōc locō
adeō	tālī modō
adhūc	ad hoc tempus, ad hunc locum
aliquandō	aliquō tempore
ante	ante hoc tempus
anteā	ante hoc tempus
antehāc	ante hoc tempus
circum	circum eum locum
citrā	cis[3] eum locum
cōram	cōram eō homine
crās	illō diē post hunc diem
cūr	quā rē
deinde	ex eō tempore
eō	ad eum locum
eōdem	ad eundem locum
extrā	extrā eum locum

---

[1] Used with numbers
[2] See §12 for definition of noun substitutor. For syntax, see p. 84.
[3] **Cis** (prep w acc), *on this side*.

Noninflected words: noun substitutors

noun substitutor	equivalent noun phrase
funditus	ā fundāmentō
herī	illō diē ante hunc diem
hīc	hōc locō
hinc	ex hōc locō, ex hōc tempore
ibī	illō locō
illīc	illō locō
illō	ad illum locum
illūc	ad illum locum
inde	ex eō locō
infrā	īnfrā eum locum
interdum	aliquō tempore
intereā	inter hās rēs
interim	inter hās rēs
intus	in eō locō
istīc	istō locō
ita	tālī modō
item	eōdem modō
iterum	secundā vice
juxtā	juxtā eum locum
mox	citō tempore
numquam	nūllō tempore
nunc	hōc tempore
nūper	paucīs ante diēbus
ōlim	tempore incertō
palam	palam eīs hominibus
paulisper	brevī tempore
post	post hās rēs
posteā	post hās rēs
prope	prope hunc locum
prōtinus	sine morā
quā	quā viā, quō itinere
quācumque	quācumque viā
quandō	quō tempore
quī	quā ratiōne
quō	quem ad locum
rursum	secundā vice
rursus	secundā vice
semper	omnī tempore
sīc	tālī modō
simul	eōdem tempore
tum	illō tempore
tunc	illō tempore

noun substitutor	equivalent noun phrase
ubī	quō locō, quō tempore
ubīcumque	quōcumque locō
ubīque	omnibus in locīs
ultrō	suā sponte
undique	ex omnibus partibus
utcumque	omnī modō

9. **Adverbs** (for syntax, see p. 84)

Formation

Latin adverbs are not inflected but are usually formed on the stem of inflected words. Most adverbs consist of an adjective stem plus the ending **-ter** or **-ē** (or rarely, **-e**).

   a. Adverbs formed on 1st and 2d decl adjs usually end in **-ē**

        jūstus → jūstē

   but sometimes end in **-e**.

        malus → male

   b. Adverbs formed on 3d decl adjs usually end in **-ter**

        fortis → fortiter

   c. Some adverbs, usually formed on a noun or participle stem, end in **-im** or **-tim**

        pars → partim
        prīvātus → prīvātim[1]

   d. Adverbial numerals based on the numbers **quīnque** and above are formed with the stem of the cardinal numeral plus the ending **-iēns**

        quīnquiēns, *five times*
        sexiēns, *six times*

   e. A few adverbs are not formed on any noun, adj, or verb base. These include **clam, persaepe, repente, saepe,** and the first four adverbial numerals, **semel, bis, ter,** and **quater.**

---

[1] Other common adverbs in **-im** used in *Artēs Latīnae* are
    certātim   interim   utrimque
    fūrtim   statim

Noninflected words: adverbs

Comparative

Adverbs have no unique comparative form. Instead, the comparative of most adverbs[1] may be expressed by using **magis**, *more,* to modify the adverb. For some of these adverbs, the comparative may also be expressed by using the neuter accusative singular form of the comparative adjective

> **clārius**, *more clearly*[2]

Superlative

The superlative of most adverbs[1] is formed either by changing the **-us-a-um** ending of the superlative of the adjective to **-ē**

> **pulcherrimus-a-um** → **pulcherrimē**
> **clārissimus-a-um** → **clārissimē**

or by using **maximē**, *most,* to modify the adverb. Some adverbs are not compared at all.

10. **Adjectivals** (for syntax, see p. 84)

> **frūgī**   **potis**   **tot**
> **mīlle**   **quot**
> **necesse** **satis/sat**

cardinal numerals 4 through 199 (see section below)

NUMERALS

Cardinal numerals answer the question: **Quot?** *How many?* Ordinal numerals answer the question: **Quotus?** *In which order?* The first three cardinal numerals, **ūnus, duo,** and **trēs,** are regular adjectives with complete declensions; all other cardinal numbers from 4 to 199 are adjectivals and thus indeclinable.[3] All ordinal numbers, such as **prīmus-a-um,** are declined like regular adjectives, with full declensions in singular and plural.

---

[1] That is, those adverbs that answer the question: *In what way?* (**Quāliter?**). See Syntax, p. 84.
[2] See p. 54 for this adverbial use of the adj.
[3] In a number like **vīgintī ūnus,** *twenty-one,* **vīgintī** is indeclinable, but **ūnus** is declined.

Declension of ūnus, duo, and trēs

ūnus			duo			trēs	
m	f	n	m	f	n	m&f	n
ūnus	ūna	ūnum	duo	duae	duo	trēs	tria
ūnum	ūnam	ūnum	duōs, duo	duās	duo	trēs, trīs	tria
ūnō	ūnā	ūnō	duōbus	duābus	duōbus	tribus	tribus
ūnī	ūnī	ūnī	duōbus	duābus	duōbus	tribus	tribus
ūnīus	ūnīus	ūnīus	duōrum	duārum	duōrum	trium	trium

	Cardinal	Ordinal	Roman
1.	ūnus-a-um, *one*	prīmus-a-um, *first*	I
2.	duo, duae, duo, *two*	secundus, *second*	II
3.	trēs, tria, *three*	tertius, *third*	III
4.	quattuor	quārtus	IIII or IV
5.	quīnque	quīntus	V
6.	sex	sextus	VI
7.	septem	septimus	VII
8.	octō	octāvus	VIII
9.	novem	nōnus	VIIII or IX
10.	decem	decimus	X
11.	ūndecim	ūndecimus	XI
12.	duodecim	duodecimus	XII
13.	tredecim	tertius decimus	XIII
14.	quattuordecim	quārtus decimus	XIIII or XIV
15.	quīndecim	quīntus decimus	XV
16.	sēdecim	sextus decimus	XVI
17.	septendecim	septimus decimus	XVII
18.	duodēvīgintī	duodēvīcēsimus	XVIII
19.	ūndēvīgintī	ūndēvīcēsimus	XVIIII or XIX
20.	vīgintī	vīcēsimus	XX
21.	vīgintī ūnus-a-um (ūnus et vīgintī)	vīcēsimus prīmus (ūnus et vīcēsimus)	XXI
22.	vīgintī duo (duo et vīgintī)	vīcēsimus secundus (alter et vīcēsimus)	XXII
30.	trīgintā	trīcēsimus	XXX
40.	quadrāgintā	quadrāgēsimus	XXXX or XL
50.	quīnquāgintā	quīnquāgēsimus	L
60.	sexāgintā	sexāgēsimus	LX
70.	septuāgintā	septuāgēsimus	LXX
80.	octōgintā	octōgēsimus	LXXX

Numerals

	Cardinal	*Ordinal*	*Roman*
90.	nōnāgintā	nōnāgesimus	LXXXX or XC
100.	centum	centēsimus	C
101.	centum (et) ūnus	centēsimus (et) prīmus	CI
120.	centum (et) vīgintī	centēsimus vīcēsimus	CXX
121.	centum vīgintī ūnus	centēsimus vīcēsimus prīmus	CXXI

The hundreds from 200 to 900 are declined

200.	ducentī-ae-a	ducentēsimus	CC
300.	trecentī-ae-a	trecentēsimus	CCC
400.	quadringentī-ae-a	quadringentēsimus	CCCC
500.	quīngentī-ae-a	quīngentēsimus	D
600.	sēscentī-ae-a	sēscentēsimus	DC
700.	septingentī-ae-a	septingentēsimus	DCC
800.	octingentī-ae-a	octingentēsimus	DCCC
900.	nōngentī-ae-a	nōngentēsimus	DCCCC

The adjectival **mīlle** is not declined, but its pl, **mīlia**, is a declinable neut noun

1,000.	mīlle	mīllēsimus	M
1,120.	mīlle centum vīgintī	mīllēsimus centēsimus vīcēsimus	MCXX
1,900.	mīlle nōngentī	mīllēsimus nōngentēsimus	MDCCCC
2,000.	duo mīlia	bis mīllēsimus	MM
10,000.	decem mīlia	deciēns mīllēsimus	X̄
100,000.	centum mīlia	centiēns mīllēsimus	C̿
1,000,000.	deciēns centēna mīlia	deciēns centiēns mīllēsimus	⌈X⌉

There are three other kinds of numerals in Latin:
Distributive numerals answer the question: **Quotēnī?** *In sets of how many?* or *How many apiece?* The first five are:

1. **singulī-ae-a**, *one apiece, singly, by ones*
2. **bīnī-ae-a**, *two apiece, in sets of two, by twos*
3. **ternī-ae-a**
4. **quaternī-ae-a**
5 **quīnī-ae-a**

Multiplicative numerals answer the question: **Quot rēbus cōnstāns?** *Consisting of how many parts?*

1. **simplex** (gen **simplicis**), *single*
2. **duplex** (gen **duplicis**), *double*
3. **triplex** (gen **triplicis**), *triple*
4. **quadruplex** (gen **quadruplicis**), *quadruple*
5. **quincuplex** (gen **quincuplicis**), *quintuple*

Adverbial numerals answer the question: **Quotiēns?** *How many times?*[1]

1. **semel**, *once*
2. **bis**, *twice*
3. **ter**, *three times*
4. **quater**, *four times*
5. **quinquiēns**, *five times*

---

[1] See p. 34.

Part II
Syntax

INTRODUCTION

Syntax is the study of how words function in their environments. The "environment" of each word is the sentence it is in; the word occupies a "slot" created or defined by this environment. In the sentence

>   **Mārtiālis patrōnum quaerit.** *Martial seeks a patron.*

the environment **patrōnum quaerit** implies a subject slot (since a transitive verb such as **quaerit**, always has a subject either expressed or implied), filled here by **Mārtiālis**. In the same way, the environment **Mārtiālis quaerit** implies a complement slot, occupied here by **patrōnum** (since a transitive verb always takes an accusative complement, of "direct object"). Finally, the environment **Mārtiālis patrōnum** implies a slot for a transitive verb, here filled by **quaerit**.

As a rule, the same slot may not be occupied by more than one construction. Thus

>   *****Mārtiālis patrōnum fāmam quaerit.**

is a non-Latin sentence because the object slot is occupied by two nouns, **patrōnum** and **fāmam**. On the other hand, the sentence

>   **Mārtiālis patrōnum trīduum quaerit.** *Martial seeks a patron for three days.*

also has two nouns in the accusative case, but they fill different slots, **patrōnum** as the object of the verb **quaerit**, and **trīduum** as a verb modifier telling "how long."

The only times that two constructions can occupy the same slot are those when they are "leveled" with one another, when in "apposition" with one another, or when in "progressive definition" with one another.

Leveling involves linking two or more constructions that occupy the same slot but that refer to different things. Usually a conjunction, such as **-que** or **et**, is used to make the link

> **Mārtiālis patrōnum fāmamque quaerit.** *Martial seeks a patron and fame.*

Latin often leaves out a coordinating conjunction where English includes it

> **Fortūna fortēs metuit, ignāvōs premit.** *Fortune fears the brave and crushes the coward.* I, 15, S41.

Apposition involves equating two or more constructions in the same slot, which refer to exactly the same thing

> **Mārtiālis poēta patrōnum quaerit.** *Martial, the poet, seeks a patron.*

Progressive definition occurs when two or more constructions occupying the same slot are parts of the same whole and serve to define each other more precisely. For example, in the sentence

> **Fēmina Rōman ad Jovis templum venit.** *The woman comes to Rome to the temple of Jupiter.*

Rōmam and **ad Jovis templum** both occupy the same slot, but **ad Jovis templum** defines more exactly what part of Rome the woman comes to.

Variant constructions

Sometimes a variety of words or constructions may be used interchangeably to fill a slot. For example, compare the two phrases

> **hōrum omnium fortissimī,** *the bravest of all these* II, 17, BG1.
> **nōbilissimus dē senātōribus,** *the noblest of the senators* LS 16, p. 130.

In the first phrase the superlative is modified by a noun in the genitive case (**omnium**); in the second phrase, it is modified by a prepositional phrase. Thus the superlative of an adjective creates a slot that can be filled by two variant constructions.

Most often the slots of subject and complement are filled by nouns or pronouns. However, a relative clause can always be used as a substitute. In the sentence

> **Absentem laedit, cum ēbriō quī lītigat.** *Who quarrels with a drunken person harms an absent person.* I, 19, S68.

the subject of **laedit** is the relative clause **cum ēbriō quī lītigat**.

Introduction

In the sentence

> **Quod nōn dedit Fortūna, nōn ēripit.** *Fortune does not take away what she has not given.* I, 27, S135.

the object of **ēripit** is the relative clause **quod nōn dedit Fortūna**.

With certain verbs, other types of clauses, such as **ut** clauses and indirect questions, may sometimes replace other constructions in the subject or complement slot. For example, the verb **volō** may take two accusative complements, of which one is a noun or pronoun and the other an infinitive.[1] Its double complement may be replaced by an **ut** clause without change in meaning, so that

> **Speculō vōs ūtī volō.** *I want you to use the mirror.* II, 15, R62.

means the same thing as

> **Volō ut speculō ūtāminī.**

Omission of items

Latin writers often leave a slot vacant when the construction filling it is understood from the context.

The same subject is regularly deleted in successive clauses or sentences, as in

> **Pauper vidērī Cinna vult. Et est pauper.** *Cinna wishes to seem poor. And he is poor.* I, 3, R8.

instead of

> **Pauper vidērī Cinna vult. Et Cinna est pauper.**

The subject is not deleted when the author wishes to emphasize it, as in

> **Nōn cēnat sine aprō noster, Tite, Caeciliānus.**
> **Bellum convīvam Caeciliānus habet.**
> *Titus, our friend Caecilianus does not dine without a boar. Caecilianus has a pretty guest.* I. 19, S62.

Subject pronouns in the 1st and 2d person (**egō, nōs; tū, vōs**) are regularly deleted. If they are included, it is for emphasis.

---

[1] See §14

The same verb is regularly omitted in successive clauses or sentences. For example

> **Ūnum oculum Thāis nōn habet; ille duōs.** *Thais is missing one eye; he is missing two.* I, 30, R8.

instead of

> **Ūnum oculum Thāis nōn habet; ille nōn habet duōs.**

The same complement is regularly omitted in successive clauses or sentences

> **Ūnum oculum Thāis nōn habet; ille duōs.**

instead of

> **Ūnum oculum Thāis nōn habet; ille duōs oculōs.**

Occasionally the *subject, object, and verb* are all omitted. For example

> **Sī meminī, fuerant tibi quattuor, Aelia, dentēs.**
> **Expulit ūna duōs tussis et ūna duōs.**
> *If I remember, Aelia, you had four teeth. One cough knocked out two teeth and another two more.* II, 6, R15.

instead of

> **Sī meminī, fuerant tibi quattuor, Aelia, dentēs.**
> **Expulit ūna duōs dentēs tussis et ūna tussis duōs dentēs expulit.**

Parts of replies to questions are regularly omitted. The answer to

> **Quis bellum convīvam habet?** *Who has an agreeable guest?*

most commonly is

> **Caeciliānus.**

rather than

> **Caeciliānus bellum convīvam habet.**

The *verb introducing a direct quotation,* such as **ait, inquit, dixit,** is often omitted

> **At ille exspīrāns: "Fortīs indignē tulī."**
> *But he said as he lay dying, "In disgrace I endured the brave ones."* II, 15, R64.

instead of

> **At ille exspīrāns ait . . .**

The linking verb <u>est</u> is frequently omitted. For example

> **Ars longa, vīta brevis.** *Art is long, life is short.* I, 17, S52.

instead of

> **Ars longa est, vīta brevis est.**

The following outline lists the classes of Latin words (nouns, verbs, etc.) and shows the ways in which different forms of these words fill different slots in the Latin sentences. The outline is intended primarily for easy reference to and review of the grammar in *Artēs Latīnae.* Additional items of interest, supplementary explanations, and minor exceptions are included in the *Advanced Notes.* As in the Morphology section, you will be referred to these *Notes* by the symbol §.

SYNTAX OF INFLECTED WORDS

As mentioned earlier[1] Latin has two kinds of words, those that are inflected (change form) and those that are not. Nouns, adjectives, pronouns, and verbs are inflected.

Nouns (for Morphology, see pp. 2-6)

Nouns are inflected for number and case.

I. Number

    A. As in English, singular number usually represents "one."
    B. As in English, plural number usually represents "more than one."
    C. However, Latin sometimes uses a singular where English uses a plural and vice versa. See §13.

II. Case

Latin is generally said to have five cases: nominative, accusative, ablative, dative, and genitive. In addition there is a vocative case for personal nouns and a locative case for a few place names. See pp. 53-54 and § 14.

---

[1] Morphology, p. 2.

A. Uses of the *nominative*

1. As the subject of a verb [1]

   Vestis **virum** reddit. *Clothes make the man.* I, 1, S1.
   Sapientia vīnō obumbrātur. *Wisdom is overshadowed by wine.* I, 12, S27.
   Nēmō sine vitiō est. *No one is without a fault.* I, 12, S26.

2. As the complement[2] of a connecting verb, such as est, fit, dīcitur, vocātur

   Oculī sunt in amōre **ducēs**. *Eyes are the leaders in love.* I, 17, S50.
   Cicerō fit **cōnsul**. *Cicero becomes consul.*
   Cicerō dīcitur **cōnsul**. *Cicero is called consul.*

   When the subject and complement are both nouns in the nominative, the statement may be ambiguous

   Vīta **vīnum** est. *Life is wine.* or *Wine is life.* I, 17, S49.

   When one nominative is a noun and the other is an adjective, the adjective is the complement

   Nēmō **līber** est. *No one is free.* I, 21, S74.

3. As a presentative nominative, which presents words independent of any larger construction, as in a title, a label, or a list of words

   Artēs Latīnae

4. In a citation, where the noun is talked about as an isolated word, as in

   Dā cāsum accūsātīvum nōminis **puella**. *Give the accusative case of the noun* **puella**.

5. As the form of the vocative. See p. 2 and p. 53.

---

[1] The subject is that part of the sentence with which the verb agrees in person and number.

[2] The complement of a verb is a word, phrase, or clause that "completes" the meaning of a verb; it must either accompany the verb or be implied. The complement of most verbs is in the acc case, and is then commonly called the direct object; but for certain verbs it may be in the nom, abl, dat, or gen case.

Inflected words: nouns

B. Uses of the *accusative*

1. As the complement (direct object) of a verb

    Vēritātem diēs aperit. *Time discloses the truth.* I, 3, S2.

    Some verbs can take two accusative complements, of which one is often personal and one nonpersonal [1]

    Sōtēria poscis **amīcōs.** *You ask your friends for presents.* II, 11, R44.

2. To modify a verb
    a. With a preposition that "governs" or "takes" the accusative.[2] Note that the entire prepositional phrase modifies the verb

    quī **trāns mare** currunt, *they who travel across the sea* I, 27, S125.

    b. Without a preposition. The accusative without a preposition is common with

    •names of towns, cities, and small islands

    •**domus** and **rūs** as the goal of verbs of motion, answering the question: *To what place?* (**Quem ad locum? Quō?**)

    eōrum quī **domum** rediērunt, *of those who returned home* II, 24, BG29.

    •Words of time to show: *How long?* (**Quam diū?**)[3]

    nostrī **triduum** morātī, *our men, delaying for a period of three days* II, 24, BG26.

---

[1] Among the verbs in *Artēs Latīnae* that take two acc are

    doceō   interrogō   ōrō   postulō   rogō
    flāgitō   jubeō   poscō   reposcō   suādeō

the **verba sentiendī**, (where one acc is an infinitive), such as

    dīcō   audiō   scrībō

and factitive verbs, verbs that make, "facit," something or someone into something or someone else, such as

    appellō   creō   exīstimō   habeō   legō   praebeō   putō
    cēnseō   dūcō   faciō   jūdicō   nōminō   praestō   reddō

See § 15 on factitive verbs.

[2] See Morphology, p. 31 for a list of these prepositions.

[3] The abl is sometimes used in the same way. See p. 48.

- Words of distance to show: *How far?* (**Quam longē?**)

    quī in longitūdinem mīlia passuum ducenta quadrāgintā patēbant, *which stretched 240 miles in length* II, 18, BG2.

- The supine after verbs of motion[1]

    simul exieris pāstum, *as soon as you go out to eat* II, 14, R57.

3. To modify a noun
    a. As part of a prepositional phrase modifying a noun

       Negat sē posse iter ūlli per Prōvinciam dare. *He said that he could not give anyone passage through the Province.* II, 21, BG8.

    b. In dates where the preposition **ante** governing the accusative is omitted but understood

       sextō Īdūs Mārtiās [short for **sextō diē ante Īdūs Mārtiās**], *on the sixth day before the Ides of March* LS17, p. 150.[2]

4. To modify an adjective (often the passive participle) to show *In what respect?* Since this usage, generally found in poetry, is an imitation of a Greek construction, it is often called the Greek accusative. It is usually used with parts of the body.

    faucēs et colla revinctus. *tied as to your throat and neck,* that is, *with your throat and neck bound* LS9 p. 65.

5. In the exclamatory accusative, an exclamation that is not part of a larger structure

    Ō mē infēlicem! *Oh, poor me!* II, 15, R63.

C. Uses of the *ablative*

1. To modify a passive verb to show "means" or "agent." See §17.
    a. **Ā/ab** is used with a personal noun to show agent

       Ā cane nōn magnō saepe tenētur aper. *A boar is often held by a small dog.* I, 11, S23.

---

[1] See p. 79.
[2] See §16 for discussion of Roman dating.

Inflected words: nouns

    b. A nonpersonal noun in the ablative without a preposition is used to show the means or instrument[1]

        Sapientia vinō obumbrātur. *Wisdom is overshadowed by wine.* I, 12, S27.

2. To modify a verb in other ways
   a. With a preposition
      •When the preposition "governs" the ablative case[2]

        Nūllā avāritia sine poenā est. *There is no greed without punishment.* I, 9, S19.

      •With **cum** when the preposition indicates accompaniment

        Sunt cōnsūmptī cum suīs. *They with their children were destroyed.* II, 14, R57.
        Vīs cum librō natāre tuō. *You want to float along with your book.* LP25, p. 155.

      •With **cum** when abstract nouns answer the question: *In what way?* (**Quō modō?**)[3]

        Cum fidē servit. *He serves faithfully.*

   b. Without a preposition. The meaning of the noun determines its use in the ablative without a preposition.
      •Nouns indicating actions or qualities may be used to answer the question: *By what means?* (**Quō auxiliō?**)

        Parva necat morsū spatiōsum vīpera taurum. *A small snake kills a large bull by a bite.* I, 10, S21.

      •Concrete nouns can answer questions such as *By what instrument?* (**Quō īnstrūmentō?**) or *By what part of the body?* (**Quō membrō?**)

        Vulpēs nōn iterum capitur laqueō. *A fox is not caught a second time by a snare.* LP11, p. 21.

      •Time words can indicate *At what time?* (**Quō tempore?**)

        quae mediō brūmae mittere mēnse solet, *which he usually sends in the middle of the month of December* II, 6, R18.

---

[1] In poetry, **ā/ab** is used on rare occasions.
[2] See Morphology, p. 31 for a list of these prepositions. At times some of them are omitted, especially in poetry.
[3] See c, p. 48.

- Time words can answer the question *For how long?* (**Quam diū?**),[1] particularly when the noun in the ablative is modified either by a number, as in

    Vīxit annis vīgintī duōbus. *He lived for twenty-two years.* LS1, p. 6.

    or by **tōtus**, as in

    Eāque tōtā nocte continenter iērunt. *And they went continuously during this entire night.* II, 24, BG26.

- Abstract nouns can show *In what respect?*

    Helvētiī reliquōs Gallōs virtūte praecēdunt. *The Helvetians surpass the rest of the Gauls in respect to their courage.* II, 17, BG1.

c. Optionally with or without a preposition
  - When the context makes the meaning of the ablative clear without a preposition, as in

    Īnsānus mediō flūmine[2] **quaerit aquam.** *The crazy person looks for water in the middle of the river.* I, 13, S32.

  - When abstract nouns answer the question: *In what way?* (**Quō modō?**) *and* are either modified, as in

    Magnā fidē servit.[3] *He serves with great fidelity.*

    or in a series, as in

    Cōnstantiā et virtūte. *With constancy and virtue.* LP9, p. 13.

3. To modify a noun[4]
  a. With a preposition
    - When the preposition "governs" the ablative case[5]

    Ūnus ferēbat fiscōs cum pecūniā. *One was carrying boxes with money.* II, 8, R27.

---

[1] The acc is used in the same way. See b, p. 45.
[2] Instead of **mediō in flūmine**, which is also possible.
[3] Instead of **magnā cum fidē**, which is also possible.
[4] This is not a frequent use of the abl, since nouns are most often modified by other nouns in the gen case.
[5] See the list of prepositions on p. 31.

Inflected words: nouns

- In stereotyped phrases, such as

    sorōrem ex mātre, *sister on his mother's side* II, 23, BG18.

- Occasionally used as a substitute for the genitive

    praeda ex torquibus, *booty of necklaces* LS21, p. 194.

    instead of

    praeda torquium

b. Without a preposition
   - When a noun describing appearance or behavior is modified by an adjective

    Neque hominēs inimicō animō temperātūrōs ab injūriā et maleficiō existimābat. *He did not think that men of unfriendly disposition would refrain from injury and harm.* II, 20 BG7.

   - When the name of a person's tribe is added as a part of his official name

    Titus Cissōnius, Quīntī fīlius, Sergiā. *Titus Cisso, son of Quintus, [of the tribe of] Sergia.* LS14, p. 113.

4. To modify adjectives denoting excellence or value

    Ille onere dīves ēminet. *Rich with his burden he stands out.* II, 8, R27.
    Neque enim praedōne marītō fīlia dīgna tua est. *For your daughter is not deserving of a bandit husband.* LS8, p. 54.
    insignis mīlitāribus et cīvīlibus rēbus, *distinguished for military and civilian accomplishments* LS24, p. 234.

5. To modify the comparative form of an adjective or adverb (or a word implying comparison, such as **anteā,** *before*)
   a. To show the object of comparison

    Vīlius argentum est aurō, virtūtibus aurum. *Silver is cheaper than gold, but gold is cheaper than virtue.* II, 9, S33.

b. To answer the question *By how much?* (**Quantō?**). In the sentence

  Multō grātius venit. *It comes more agreeably by much.* or *It comes much more agreeably.* II, 9, S38.

  multō shows how much more agreeably.

6. As an ablative absolute: two or more words in the ablative, most commonly a noun and a perfective passive participle, which do not directly modify anything in the sentence. Generally, they show the circumstance under which the rest of the sentence occurs.

  sīc est locūtus, **partibus factīs**, leō, *thus the lion said, when the division was made* II, 12, R50.

  The imperfective active participle is less common

  hīs rēgnantibus annus ūnus complētās est, *while they were ruling, one year was completed* LS14, p. 109.

  It is commonly used without any participle with names of consuls in dates

  Lūciō Pīsōne, Aulō Gabīniō cōnsulibus, *Lucius Piso and Aulus Gabinius being consuls,* or *in the consulship of Lucius Piso and Aulus Gabinius* II, 20, BG6.

7. As a verb complement; a very small number of verbs regularly take an ablative complement [1]

  Speculō vōs ūtī volō. *I want you to use the mirror.* II, 15, R62.

D. Uses of the *dative*
  1. As the complement of a verb
    a. Some verbs regularly take one complement only in the dative[2]

      Ingrātus ūnus **omnibus miserīs** nocet. *One ungrateful person harms all miserable persons.* I, 21, S76.

---

[1] Examples of these verbs in the Basic Text are **ūtor, fruor,** and **potior. Egeō** and **careō** occur in *Lēctiōnēs Secundae.*

[2] Examples of verbs that take a complement only in the dat:

cōnfīdō	fīdō	oboediō	occurrō	placeō	serviō
conveniō	noceō	obsequor	parcō	praesum	succēdō
faveō	nūbō	obtemperō	pāreō	prōsum	

Inflected words: nouns

  b. Some verbs permit or require an indirect object in the dative in addition to a direct object in the accusative[1]

  Inopī beneficium bis dat quī dat celeriter. *He who gives quickly to a poor man gives a benefit twice.* I, 20, S70.

  c. Many compound verbs with certain prefixes[2] take the dative as a second complement

  Impōnit fīnem sapiēns et rēbus honestīs. *The wise person puts a limit even to honorable endeavors.* I, 21, S78.

2. To modify certain adjectives to indicate their point of reference[3]

   Dīs proximus ille est quem ratiō, nōn īra, movet. *He is near the gods whom reason, and not anger, moves.* I, 21, S75.

3. To indicate agent
   a. Regularly with the gerundive

   Caesar nōn exspectandum sibi statuit. *Caesar decided that waiting should not be done by him.* II, 21, BG11.

   b. Sometimes with passive verbs, particularly in poetry

   Nec sōl mihi cernitur ūllus. *And no sun is seen by me.* LS15, p. 126.

4. To indicate the point of reference (usually a person) to whom the sentence applies

   Esse tibi vērās crēdis amīcitiās? *Do you believe that you can have true friendships?* II, 2, R6.

---

[1] Some of the verbs in *Artēs Latīnae* that take indirect objects in addition to direct objects are

āscrībō	dīcō	ignōscō	nūntiō	persuādeō	renūntiō
attribuō	dō	imperō	offerō	polliceor	scrībō
crēdō	dōnō	mandō	ostendō	prōmittō	suādeō

[2] The most common prefixes occurring in such constructions are

| ad- | con- | inter- | post- | sub- |
| ante- | in- | ob- | prae- | super- |

[3] Among the adjs used in this way with the dat in *Artēs Latīnae* are

| aptus | grātus | idōneus | proprius | proximus | similis |

5. Double dative. This consists of two nouns in the dative; one noun expresses purpose,[1] the other indicates the point of reference (usually a person) to which the purposive or dative or the whole sentence applies.[2] In the sentence

>   **Patrōnus servum <u>auxiliō clientī</u> mīsit.** *The patron sent the slave as a help for the client.* II, 16.

> **auxiliō** expresses purpose (it is equivalent to a purpose clause like **(servum) quī clientem adjuvāret**), while **clientī** is the person for whom the action of the sentence was accomplished.

6. In dedicatory inscriptions, independent of any larger construction

>   **Dīs Mānibus.** *To the spirits of the Lower World*[3]   LS2, p. 15.

E. Uses of the *genitive*

1. As a verb complement
   a. With a very few verbs that may regularly pattern with the genitive[4]

   >   **Reminīscerētur veteris incommodī populī Rōmānī.** *Let him remember the ancient misfortune of the Roman people.* II, 22, BG13.

   b. With **est, habeō,** and **aestimō** when they pattern with a few nouns which show value[5]

   >   **Tantī nōn est perīre.**[6] *To die is not of that much value.* or *It isn't worth that much to die.* II, 10, R37.
   >   **cujus auctōritās <u>magnī</u> habēbātur,** *whose prestige was considered high*   LS24, p. 241.
   >   **Nūlla possessiō <u>plūris</u> quam virtūs aestimanda.** *No possession should be valued more than virtue.* LS21, p. 196.

---

[1] In English translations the purposive nature of this noun is sometimes not expressed.
     Ducēs mihī <u>auxiliō</u> fuēre. *The leaders were an aid to me.* II, 16.
[2] See point 4 above.
[3] Presumably derived from a phrase like **Hoc sepulchrum sacrum est dīs mānibus.** *This tomb is sacred to the spirits of the Lower World.*
[4] Those in *Artēs Latīnae* include **meminī, reminīscor, oblīvīscor,** and **potior. Meminī, reminīscor,** and **oblīvīscor** may optionally take the acc; **potior** may optionally take the abl.
[5] Nouns which show value are words like **multī, parvī,** and **tantī**.
[6] Presumably derived from a phrase like **Tantī mercēs nōn est perīre.** *Dying is not a reward of that much value.*

Inflected words: nouns

c. Whan a few nouns describing a crime or punishment are used with a few verbs meaning "accuse," "convict," or "condemn"

ā dictātōre <u>capitis</u> damnātus, *condemned to loss of civil rights by the dictator* [1]
LS16, p. 132.

2. To modify nouns. See § 18.

Vīta <u>hominis</u> brevis est. *The life of man is brief.* I, 22, S85.

3. To modify adjectives
   a. With certain adjectives that regularly pattern with the genitive[2]

   virtūtis expers, *lacking in courage* II, 16, R66.

   b. In the plural with the superlative form of adjectives

   <u>Hōrum omnium</u> fortissimi sunt Belgae. *The bravest of all [of] these are the Belgians.*
   II, 17, BG1.

F. Use of the *vocative:* to address directly a person (or animal or inanimate object momentarily considered a person). Unlike slots for other noun cases, the vocative slot is independent of the rest of the sentence. It may be inserted at any point in another structure and has only one meaning. See § 13.

   Mentītur qui tē vitiōsum, <u>Zōile</u>, dīcit. *He who says that you are vicious, Zoilus, is telling a lie.* II, 2, R5.

---

[1] Presumably derived from a phrase like
   ā dictātōre jūdiciō capitis damnātus, *condemned by the dictator with the punishment of [loss of] civil rights*
The noun for the crime or punishment is omitted but understood.

[2] Among the adjs that pattern with the gen in *Artēs Latīnae* are
   experiēns   immemor   memor   perītus   prōvidus
   expers   imperītus nescius plēnus
In poetry this use of the gen extends to many other adjs.

G. Use of the *locative:* to modify the verb to answer the question *Where?* (**Quō locō?**) or, more rarely *When?* (**Quō tempore?**). The locative occurs only in a very few nouns of place and time[1] and in the names of cities and islands that are singular and of the first and second declensions.

>**Domī** cēnat. *He is dining at home.* II, 10, R36.

Adjectives (for morphology, see pp. 6-10)

I. Functions in the Latin sentence

  A. They may modify nouns, as in

>**Cautus** metuit foveam lupus. *A cautious wolf fears the pitfall.* I, 6, S8.

  where **cautus** modifies **lupus**. Sometimes they modify a deleted subject, as in

>Trahimur **omnēs** studiō laudis. *We are all impelled by a desire for praise.* II, 10, S40.

  where **omnēs** modifies a deleted **nōs**.

  B. They may be used as nouns, as in

>**Īnsānus** mediō flūmine quaerit aquam. *The crazy person seeks water in the middle of the river.* I, 13, S32.

  where **īnsānus** takes the place of a noun for a person.

  C. The accusative neuter singular form of a few adjectives may substitute for an adverb in certain circumstances.

    1. The accusative neuter singular forms **facile, impūne, rēctum, primum,** and **quid** may be used adverbially

>nē **rēctum** posset aspicere, *so that he could not see properly* LS16, p. 132.
>quī **primum** eōs vīcit, *who conquered them for the first time*[2] LS15, p. 122.
>**Quid** ita cessā'runt pedēs? *Why did your feet stop?* or *What did your feet stop for?* II, 7, R25.

---

[1] See §2.

[2] This use of **primum** to mean *for the first time* contrasts with the use of the nom, **primus,** as in **Primus** eōs vīcit. *He was the first to conquer them.*

Inflected words: adjectives

2. The accusative neuter singular form of a few adjectives of quantity, like **multum**, may be used adverbially to show *How much?* (**Quantum?**)

Multum falleris. *You are much mistaken.* II, 14, R58.

3. The accusative neuter singular comparative form of adjectives may be used to express the comparative of adverbs[1]

Multō grātius venit. *It comes in much more welcome fashion.* II, 9, S38.

D. The accusative neuter singular form of a few adjectives may be used as other parts of speech

1. The accusative neuter singular form of **vērus** may serve as a sentence connector

Vērum perītīs irritōs tendit dolōs. *But he stretches his snares in vain for experienced people.* II, 14, R58.

2. The accusative neuter singular form of **uter** may be used as an interrogative to ask which of two statements is true

Utrum vir an elephantus est? *Which is it, a man or an elephant?*

3. The accusative neuter singular form of the interrogative adjective, **quod**, may be used as a subordinating conjunction.
   a. With a pronoun as antecedent

Hoc scio, quod scrībit nūlla puella tibi. *I know this, the fact that no girl writes to you.* II, 6, R17.

   b. More often without an antecedent

Rumpitur invidiā quīdam quod[2] mē Rōma legit. *A certain person is bursting with envy because Rome is reading me.* II, 10, R35.

---

[1] See the comparative of adverbs, p. 35.
[2] **Quod** here is short for **eō quod**, *for this reason, that.*

II. Adjectives are inflected for number, case, and gender,[1] and those used to modify nouns agree with them in these three respects. Gender is determined in the following manner:

A. For adjectives that modify nouns: the most important determinant of the gender of the adjective is the declension of the noun it modifies, as shown in the table below.

	Noun declension				
	1st	2d	3d	4th	5th
Usual gender	fem	masc	masc fem	masc	fem
Gender when nom = acc sg		neut	neut	neut	

Major modifications:

1. The gender of many 3d declension nouns can be predicted from the suffix. The following are the most common:

Gender	Suffix	Example
Usually masculine	-or -es (gen -itis)	honor mīles
Usually feminine	-tūs -tās -iō -ēs -dō	virtūs fēlīcitās ōrātiō caedēs harundō

---

[1] Nouns in Latin are grouped into three gender classes: "masculine," "feminine," and "neuter." These classes determine which of three possible forms a modifying adj must take for a given case and number.

Inflected words: adjectives

2. The gender of personal nouns and proper names of people usually reflects the person's actual sex, regardless of the noun's declension. The same is true for names of animals used as personal nouns. The point is illustrated in the following table.[1]

	Examples	Decl	Expected gender of decl	Actual gender
Male personal nouns and names	poēta nauta agricola Porsenna	1st	f	m
Female personal nouns and names	Erōtion[2]	2d	n	f
	Thāis	3d	m or f	f
	anus	4th	m or n	

---

[1] The following are some exceptions: **vulpēs,** *fox* (always fem, even when referring to a male); **pāvō,** *peacock* (always masc); **rāna,** *frog* (always fem); **caput,** *head, human being* (always neut).

[2] **Erōtion** is a Greek form of a 2d decl neut noun; such nouns, when used as women's names, are neut in form (nom/acc alike) but take adjs in the fem gender.

3. The gender of a noun that falls into the same generic class is sometimes determined by the class rather than by the noun's declension, as shown in the table below.

Class	Example	Decl	Expected gender of decl	Actual gender
winds rivers	Aquilō Tiberis	3d	m or f	m
plants and trees	laurus quercus	2d 4th	m m	f
cities	Corinthus Carthāgō	2d 3d	m m or f	
islands	Rhodos Vectis	2d 3d	m m or f	
countries	Aegyptus	2d	m	

4. Miscellaneous exceptions. The following feminine nouns do not fit into any of the above categories: **manus, domus, porticus, Īdūs, tribus** (all 4th declension) and **humus** (2d declension). **Diēs** is also exceptional because it is masculine in the plural but may be masculine or feminine in the singular. Some nouns have "common gender," that is, they may be either masculine or feminine, depending on the sex of the person or animal referred to: **convīva, exul, canis,** etc.

B. For adjectives used as nouns, gender is determined as follows:

1. The masculine form of adjectives is used to represent males or people in general

> **Īnsānus mediō flūmine quaerit aquam.** *The crazy person seeks water in the middle of the river.* I, 13, S32.
> **Stultī timent Fortūnam, sapientēs ferunt.** *Stupid people fear Fortune, (but) wise people endure her.* I, 15, S42.

2. The feminine form of adjectives is used to represent females

> **Quisquis amat luscam, luscam putat esse venustam.** *Whoever loves a one-eyed woman thinks that a one-eyed woman is beautiful.* LS2, p. 13.

Inflected words: pronouns

3. The neuter form of adjectives is used to represent things or abstractions

Magna dī cūrant, **parva** neglegunt. *The gods take care of large things but neglect small things.* I, 16, S46.
Dīc **vērum** mihi. *Tell me the truth.* LS21, p. 191.

Pronouns (for morphology, see pp. 10-14)

I. Personal pronouns

A. They are used in place of nouns. In the sentence

Tē, Line, nōn videō. *I do not see you, Linus.* II, 6, R16.

the **tē** replaces **Linum**.

B. When used as the subject of a sentence, the personal pronoun of the 1st or 2d person is regularly deleted, though it may be retained for the purpose of emphasis. In the sentence

Omnia vincit Amōr; et **nōs** cēdāmus Amōrī. *Love conquers all; let us, too, yield to Love.* II, 4, S25.

the pronoun **nōs**, *us* is emphasized.

C. When used as the subject of a sentence, the personal pronoun of the 3d person is also regularly deleted. It is retained, however, either for emphasis or when the subject it stands for is not the subject of the preceding sentence.

D. When a pronoun in a clause refers to the same person as the subject of the clause, the reflexive pronoun is used

Sē sōlum Labiēnus amat. *Labienus loves himself alone.* II, 1, R1.

E. The personal pronoun for the 3d person, **is**, may also be used as an adjective meaning an unemphatic *this, that, these, those*

Aquitānia ad Pyrēnaeōs montēs et **eam** partem Ōceanī quae est ad Hispāniam pertinet. *Aquitania stretches to the Pyrenees Mountains and to that part of the Atlantic which is near Spain.* II, 17, BG1.

II. Other pronouns

A. They may be used in place of nouns (hence the term "pronoun")

Nōn omnēs **eadem** mīrantur amantque. *Not all people admire and like the same things.* II, 1, S4.

B. They may be used as adjectives to modify nouns

> Ascrībere hoc dēbēbunt exemplum sibi. *They ought to apply this example to themselves.* II, 7, R22.

1. Determinative pronoun and adjective: **idem**
   a. As a pronoun it means *the same one*

   > Difficilis, facilis, jūcundus, acerbus es idem. *You, the same person, are hard to get along with, easy to get along with, pleasant, and unpleasant.* I, 30, R11.

   b. As an adjective it means *the same*

   > Et idem inventus māne est mortuus Andragorās. *And the same Andragoras was found dead in the morning.* I, 30, R12.

2. Intensifying pronoun and adjective: **ipse**
   a. As a pronoun, it refers to an important word in an earlier clause or expresses the idea of *that very person we were talking about*

   > Ipsum vidimus. *We saw that very person.*

   b. As an adjective it intensifies the noun it modifies

   > Puer ipse currit. *The boy is running.* or *The boy himself is running.*

3. Demonstrative pronouns and adjectives: **hic, ille, iste**

   hic
   a. As a pronoun referring to *the one(s) near the speaker,* **hic** is often equivalent to the English *this one (these ones)* and by extension, *he, she, it, they.* It may also mean *the second of two people or things mentioned,* like the English *the latter*

   > Hocc emis. *You bought it.* I, 29, R6.

   b. As an adjective referring to *the one(s) near the speaker,* it means *this (these)*

   > In hōc signō vincēs. *In this sign you will conquer.* I, 26, S120.

ille

a. As a pronoun referring to *the one(s) away from the speaker*, **ille** is often equivalent to the English *that one (those ones)* and by extension, *he she, it, they*. It may also mean *the first of two people or things mentioned*, like English *the former*

Hocc illis dictum est quibus honōrem et glōriam Fortūna tribuit. *This was said to those to whom Fortune has given honor and glory.* II, 7, R24.

b. As an adjective referring to *the one(s) away from the speaker*, it means *that (those)*

Hic canis est parvus, sed ille canis est magnus. *This dog is small, but that dog is big.*

iste

a. As a pronoun it refers to *that thing (or person or remark) which is nearest the person spoken to.* It often means *that one of yours*

Dīcis formōsam, dīcis tē, Bassa, puellam.
Istud, quae nōn est, dīcere, Bassa, solet.
You say, Bassa, that you are a pretty young girl.
The woman who isn't, Bassa, usually says that [which you just said]. II, 2, R3.

b. As an adjective referring to *the one(s) near the person spoken to*, **iste** is often equivalent to the English *your*

Istum cibum ede. *Eat that food near you.* or *Eat your food.*

Sometimes **iste** has contemptuous connotations

Istud cōnsilium nōbis nocuit. *That fool plan [of yours] harmed us.*

4. Relative pronoun and interrogative adjective: **quī**
   a. As a pronoun

   •When it introduces a relative (subordinate) clause, which modifies a noun or pronoun in the main clause, **quī** means *who, which* or *what*. It may also be used to substitute for **is, hic,** or **ille**, and these serve to connect closely the sentence it is in with the preceding sentence; in this case it functions as a "coordinating relative" pronoun.

In both instances **qui** agrees in gender and number with its antecedent noun or pronoun but takes its case from its use in its own clause. In the sentence

Dīs proximus ille est quem ratiō, nōn īra movet. *He is near the gods whom reason, not anger, moves.* I, 21, S75.

quem is masculine singular because it refers to **ille**; it is in the accusative case because it is the object of the verb of the subordinate clause, **movet**.

•Although not inflected for person, **qui** may be used for all three persons.

1st person
Quā rē ego nōn sūdō, qui tēcum, Zōile, cēnō? *Why don't I perspire, Zoilus, who am dining with you?* II, 16, R71.
2d person
Qui modo sēcūrus nostra irridēbās mala. *You who, when safe, were just now ridiculing my misfortunes.* II, 7, R25.
3d person
Qui dedit beneficium taceat. *Let the one who has given a benefit keep silent.* II, 4, S29.

•**Qui** is regularly the first word in its clause, although a word or words may be placed ahead of it in the same clause for emphasis.

odōrem quae jūcundum lātē spargeret, *which spread far and wide a pleasing odor* II, 13, R52.

    b. As an interrogative adjective it means *Which? What? What kind of?* but this use is rather rare

Quae ratiō est? *What's the reason?* I, 18, S61.

5. Interrogative pronoun and adjective: **quis**
    a. As a pronoun
      •It introduces direct and indirect questions and agrees in gender, number, and case with the noun or pronoun it asks for [1]

Quid mihi reddat ager quaeris, Line, Nōmentānus? *You ask, Linus, what profit does the farm at Nomentanus give me?* II, 6, R16.
Simili quaesivit modō quis major esset. *She asked in a similar way who was larger.* II, 9, R28.

---

[1] **Quis?** *Who?* asks for a personal noun; **Quid?** *Which? What?* asks for a nonpersonal noun.

Inflected words: verbs

• It regularly is the first word in its clause. Words may precede it in the same clause to receive emphasis

Nescio tam multīs quid scrībās Fauste, puellīs. *I don't know, Faustus, what you write to so many girls.* II, 6, R17.

   b. **Quis, quid** is used only rarely as the interrogative adjective; the more usual form is **quī, quae, quad** (identical with the relative pronoun).

Verbs (for morphology, see pp. 14-29)

Verbs are inflected (change form) for person, number, voice, mood, tense, and aspect.

I. The verbal category of person indicates whether the subject is the speaker by himself (1st singular) or with others (1st plural); whether it is the person or persons addressed (2d singular or plural); or whether it is someone or something else (3d singular or plural).

   A. As in English, most Latin verbs can take a subject in any of the three persons.

   B. A few verbs, called "impersonal," have a form only in the 3d person singular and do not take a noun subject.[1] Instead, the subject must be either an infinitive, an **ut** clause with the subjunctive, a relative clause, or **id** substituting for any one of these but never standing for a noun.

   Semel in annō licet insānīre *It is permitted to be crazy once a year.* II, 19, S76.
   Ēvēnit tamen ut victōrēs cōnsulēs ambō morerentur. *But it turned out that both victorious consuls were killed.* LS24, p. 228.
   Quod licet Jovī nōn licet bovī. *What is permitted to Jupiter is not permitted to the ox.* II, 19, S77.

   But note that a noun may never be the subject of an impersonal verb

   *****Vīnum licet.** *Wine is permitted.*

---

[1] These verbs also have forms for the infinitive, but never for the 1st or 2d person sg and pl or the 3d person pl. Among the impersonal verbs in *Artēs Latīnae* are
   addecet   libet   oportet   piget   rēfert
   decet   licet   paenitet   pudet
In addition, certain verbs that have forms in the 1st and 2d persons and that take noun subjects may also be used in the same way as impersonal verbs. Examples are
   accidit   ēvenit   placet
   cōnstat   fit
Often the lexical meaning of the verb differs in the two uses: **accidō** means *I fall down* but the impersonal **accidit** means *it happens*.

C. The subject of imperatives (the command forms of a verb) is 2d person (**tū** or **vōs**) but is regularly deleted. When not deleted, it adds emphasis. In the sentence

>**<u>Audī</u>, <u>vidē</u>, <u>tacē</u>, si vīs vīvere in pāce.** *Listen, look, and be quiet if you wish to live in peace.* II, 11, S45.

tū is deleted. In the sentence

>**Dum Fāta sinunt, <u>vīvite</u> laetī.** *Live happily, while the Fates permit.* II, 14, S55.

laetī modifies a deleted **vōs**.

II. The verb agrees with its subject in *number*. Unlike English, Latin has two separate forms of the verb for the two 2d person subjects "you" (singular) and "you" (plural).

III. *Voice* tells whether the verb is active or passive, that is whether the verb's subject performs the action of the verb or is acted upon.

A. Transitive verbs have forms in both active and passive voice. See § 15.

>Active: **Diem nox <u>premit</u>.** *Night pursues day.* I, 8, S16.
>Passive: **Diēs nocte <u>premitur</u>.** *Day is pursued by night.*

B. Transitival verbs[1] do not have a passive voice, but are able to substitute for a transitive verb in an active sentence

>**Diem nox <u>sequitur</u>.** *Night follows day.*

C. Intransitive verbs
  •usually do not have passive forms (but see below, p. 65)
  •cannot substitute for transitive verbs in a sentence because they cannot take a complement in the accusative, i.e. a direct object[2]

  1. Most intransitive verbs take no complement, like **rubeō** in

  >**Rubet quīdam.** *A certain person blushes.* I, 29, R5.

---

[1] The most common are **faciō, volō**, and deponent verbs that take direct objects.
[2] A few normally intransitive verbs may occasionally take an object. **Flēre,** *weep* is usually intransitive, but in the clause
>**cāsūs cum <u>flēret</u> suōs,** *when he was bewailing his misfortunes* II, 8, R27.

it is used as a transitive verb.

Inflected words: verbs

2. Some intransitive verbs can take a complement
   - in the nominative, like **sum** and **fīo**
   - in the ablative, like **ūtor**
   - in the dative, like **placeō**
   - in the genitive, like **reminīscor**

3. A few intransitive verbs may be used in the 3d person singular passive without a subject (when it is not important to express who or what is doing the action). This construction is called the "impersonal passive."

   Rōmae <u>rēgnātum est</u> per septem rēgēs. *Ruling was done at Rome by seven kings.* LS14, p. 112.
   Nēminī <u>parcētur</u>. *Sparing will be done to no one.* or *No one will be spared.* LS4, p. 30[1].

D. The *voice* of a verb and the *form* of a verb do not always correspond.

   1. Deponent verbs are active in voice although their endings are identical, with regular passive endings. Deponents may be either transitival

      <u>Sequitur</u> superbia formam. *Conceit follows beauty.* II, 1, S7.

      or intransitive

      Ē viperā rursum vipera <u>nāscitur</u>. *A snake is born in turn from (another) snake.* II, 1, S6.

   2. A few verbs have both active and passive forms, both of which are active in meaning

      lacrimō, *I weep*
      lacrimor, *I weep*

---

[1] This is a transformation of a sentence like
   Mors nēminī parcet. *Death will spare no one.*
Note that the dat complement remains when the verb is transformed, in contrast to the acc complement of transitive verbs, which becomes the subject when the verb is transformed to the passive.

3. Semideponent verbs are those few verbs[1] that have active forms in the imperfective system and deponent forms in the perfective system, all with active voice.

   Imperfective form: **gaudeō,** *I rejoice*
   Perfective form: **gavīsus sum,** *I rejoiced*

Thus voice in verbs may be schematized as follows:

Class	Form	Voice	Example
1.	-ō	active	**teneō,** *I hold*
	-or	passive	**teneor,** *I am held*
2.	-ō	always active	**lacrimō,** *I weep*
	-or	(no contrast)	**lacrimor,** *I weep*
3.	-ō	active	**rubeō,** *I blush*
	—	—	—
4.	—	—	—
	-or	deponent	**sequor,** *I follow*
5.	-ō (imperfective)	active	**gaudeō,** *I rejoice*
	-us sum (perfective)	deponent	**gavīsus sum,** *I rejoiced*

Verbs of Class 1 (where form corresponds clearly with voice) are the most common.

IV. *Mood* tells whether the verb expresses a fact, a command, an obligation, a wish, or a possibility.

   A. The Indicative expresses fact in both main and subordinate clauses

      1. It may present a statement as either a positive or a negative fact

         Vestis virum reddit. *Clothes make the man.* I, 1, S1.
         Elephantus nōn capit mūrem. *An elephant doesn't catch a mouse.* I, 4, S5.

---

[1] There are only four semideponent verbs in *Artēs Latīnae:*
   audeō/ausus sum   **fīdō/fīsus sum**
   gaudeō/gavīsus sum **soleō/solitus sum**

Inflected words: verbs

2. It may ask a question about a fact

   Quid virum reddit? *What makes a man?*
   Redditne vestis virum? *Do clothes make the man?*

B. The imperative is the mood of command[1]

   Dīc, Postume, dē tribus capellīs. *Speak, Postumus, about the three goats.* II, 11, R45.

C. The subjunctive in *main* clauses expresses non-fact: either a wish, an obligation, or a possibility[2]

   1. A subjunctive in the negative is accompanied either by **nē** to indicate a wish

      Ignem ignī nē addās. *I wish you would not add fire to fire.* LS4, p. 28.

      or by **nōn** to indicate obligation or possibility. Since **nōn** is used to signal both obligation and possibility, the context must indicate which one is meant

      Nōn culpēs quod mūtārī nōn potest. *You ought not to blame what cannot be changed.* or *You may (possibly) not blame what cannot be changed.*

   2. If a subjunctive verb in the main clause is in the affirmative, the context (usually) provides the only clue as to whether the verb expresses wish, obligation, or possibility

      Nōs cēdāmus Amōrī. *I wish we could yield to Love.*[3] or *We ought to yield to Love.* or *It is possible we may yield to Love.* II, 4, S25.

      Modification of this rule: **utinam** may be used to show that the subjunctive is expressing a wish

      Tābēscās utinam, Sabelle, bellē. *Would that you would waste nicely away, Sabellus.* LS 24, p. 238.

   3. The choice of subjunctive forms conveys information about the conditions surrounding a wish
      a. The present imperfective subjunctive (#8) form shows a wish or hope which may yet be fulfilled

         Utinam dīves sim. *I hope to be rich.*

---

[1] But see pp. 93-94 for alternative ways to express direct command.
[2] However, the subjunctive may show fact in certain subordinate clauses. See D 1, p. 68.
[3] Or, still expressing a wish, *Let us yield to Love.*

b. The past imperfective subjunctive (#7) form shows a wish impossible to fulfill at the present time

Utinam dīves essem. *I wish that I were rich* (but I am not).

c. The past perfective subjunctive (#9) form shows a wish that was not fulfilled in the past

Utinam dīves fuissem. *I wish that I had been rich* (but I wasn't).

D. The subjunctive in a subordinate clause is used either to show fact (simply reinforcing the subordinate nature of the clause) or to show nonfact.
  1. To show fact and reinforce the subordinate nature of the clause
     a. In **cum** clauses when the **cum** means "because," "since," or "although"[1]

     Nīl bene cum faciās, faciās tamen omnia bene. *Although you do nothing well, still you do everything cleverly.* II, 6, R21.

     b. In indirect questions

     Nescio tam multīs quid scrībās puellīs. *I don't know what you write to so many girls.* II, 6, R17.

     c. In **ut** (or negative, **ut nōn**) clauses to show result [2]

     Arar in Rhodanum īnfluit incrēdibilī lēnitāte, ita ut oculīs, in utram partem fluat, jūdicārī nōn possit. *The Arar flows into the Rhone with such unbelievable slowness that it cannot be judged by the eye in which direction it is flowing.* II, 21, BG12.

     d. Where the **ut** (or **ut nōn**) clause is the subject of impersonal verbs, such as **licet, fit, ēvenit,** and **accidit**

     Hīs rēbus fīēbat ut minus lātē vagārentur. *For these reasons it happened that they wandered less widely.* II, 18, BG2.

---

[1] **Cum** takes the indicative when it means *whenever*. See II.A.2, p. 80.
[2] A word in the main clause like

       ita   tālis   tantus
       sīc   tam

signals that the **ut** clause is a result clause, not a purpose clause.

Inflected words: verbs

e. In a clause beginning with **quin** when **quin** means *but that* or comes after an expression of doubt

Nemo est tam fortis quin rei novitāte perturbētur. *No one is so brave but that he is disturbed by the novelty of a situation.* II, 19, S74.

f. With the subordinating conjunction **licet**, *although*

licet ūsque vocēs mittāsque rogēsque, *although you constantly invite me and send [slaves] to me and ask me* II, 10, R42.

2. To show nonfact
   a. In **ut** (or **nē**) clauses to show purpose[1]

   Nōn ut edam vīvō. *I do not live in order to eat.* II, 5, S31.

   in contrast to the indicative

   Nōn ut edō vīvō. *I do not live the way [as] I eat.*

   b. In an **ut** (or **nē**) clause which is the object of a transitive verb of asking, advising, commanding, etc.[2]

   Exigis ut nostrōs dōnem tibī libellōs. *You ask that I give you my books.* II, 5, R11.

   in contrast to the indicative

   Exigis ut nostrōs dōnō tibī libellōs. *While I give you my books, you ask (for something).*

   With some of these verbs the **ut** may sometimes be omitted

   Solvās cēnseō crēditōrī. *I advise you to pay [money] to your creditor.* II, 5, R12.

---

[1] Sometimes a relative clause is used in purpose clauses in place of **ut**. See 2c, p. 70 and p. 89.
[2] Examples of these verbs in *Artēs Latīnae* include

cēnseō	imperō	persuādō	rogō
cōnstituō	moneō	petō	statuō

c. In a relative clause to show either possibility

Nīl istic quod agat tertia tussis habet. *A third cough has nothing which it could do there.* II, 5, R15.

in contrast to the indicative

Nīl istic quod agit tertia tussis habet. *A third cough has nothing which it is doing there.*

or purpose

Equitātum praemittit quī videant quās in partīs hostēs iter faciant. *He sent the cavalry ahead to observe [who were to observe] in what direction the enemy was marching.* II, 23, BG15.

in contrast to the indicative

Equitātum praemittit quī vident quās in partīs hostēs iter faciant. *He sent ahead the cavalry who were observing in what direction the enemy was marching.*

d. With **dum** to show possibility

Ut spatium intercēdere posset, dum mīlitēs convenīrent, lēgātīs respondit. *So that time might intervene, until his soldiers could assemble, he replied to the ambassadors.* II, 20, BG7.

in contrast to the indicative

dum mīlitēs conveniunt, *while his soldiers were assembling.*[1]

or when **dum** means *provided that*

Dum modo sit dīves, barbarus ipse placet. *Provided he is rich, even a barbarian pleases people.* LS20, p. 184.

in contrast to the indicative

Dum est dīves, barbarus ipse placet. *While he is rich, even a barbarian pleases people.*

---

[1] When **dum** means *while*, it usually patterns with the #2 tense (as with **conveniunt** here) even when the action is in past tense.

Inflected words: verbs

e. In the subordinate clauses of an indirect statement.[1]
In the sentence

Caesar dīxit Orgetorigem, quī magnā auctōritāte esset, clientīs suōs coēgisse. *Caesar said that Orgetorix, who (Caesar added) possessed great influence, had gathered his clients.*

the **quī** clause is part of what Caesar said. By contrast, the indicative used in the same clause would mean that the **quī** clause is not part of what Caesar said but is an insertion by the speaker or writer of what he considers to be a fact

Caesar dīxit Orgetorigem, quī magnā auctōritāte erat, clientīs suōs coēgisse. *Caesar said that Orgetorix* (Editor's note: *Orgetorix possessed great influence*) *had gathered his clients.*

f. In relative clauses that express a characteristic of the person or thing referred to; this is called the subjunctive of characteristic

[Amphora] odōrem quae jūcundum lātē spargeret, *[A jar] (of the sort) which gave off a pleasant odor everywhere* II, 13, R52. See § 19.

V. Tense

A. In the indicative and the independent subjunctive, tense tells the time when the action of the verb occurs in relation to the time the speaker is talking. There are three tenses in Latin: past, present, and future. There are two different aspects for each tense, the imperfective and the perfective.[2]

Aspect	Past tense	Present tense	Future tense
	Indicative		
imperfective	#1 amābat	#2 amat[3]	#3 amābit
perfective	#4 amāverat	#5 amāvit[3]	#6 amāverit
	Subjunctive		
imperfective	#7 amāret	#8 amet	
perfective	#9 amāvisset	#10 amāverit	

---

[1] See C, p. 91.
[2] See Aspect, p. 75.
[3] Often used as narrative tenses. See p. 75, fn 1 and 2.

B. The tense of the subjunctive in a dependent clause is determined by the tense of the verb in the main clause.
1. Main verb in the indicative. When the main verb is in the indicative, the tense of the dependent subjunctive is determined by the rules of "Sequence of Tenses," which operate as follows:
    a. If the main verb is past tense (#1 or #4), then the subordinate subjunctive will also be past tense (#7 or #9). If the action of the subjunctive takes place *before* that of the main verb, the #9 subjunctive form is used; otherwise, the #7 form appears.[1]
    Main verb #1, subordinate verb #7:

    Cum mē captārēs, mittēbās mūnera nōbīs. *When you were pursuing me, you used to send me gifts.* II, 11, R46.

    Main verb #4, subordinate verb #9:

    Cum dēcidisset vulpēs in puteum, dēvēnit hircus sitiēns in eundem locum. *When a fox had fallen into a well a thirsty goat came to the same place.* II, 12, R51.

    b. If the main verb is *present or future tense* (#2, #3, #5, or #6), then the subordinate subjunctive will be present tense (#8 or #10). If the action of the subjunctive takes place *before* that of the main verb, the #10 subjunctive is used; otherwise the #8 form appears.[1]
    Main verb #2, subordinate verb #8:

    Scīs quid velit. *You know what he wants.* II, 6, R19.

    Main verb #2, subordinate verb #10:

    Quamvīs per multōs cuculus cantāverit annōs, dīcere nescit adhūc aliud verbum nisi "Cuccūc." *Although the cuckoo has sung for many years, he still doesn't know how to say any word except "Cuckoo."* LS15, p. 123.

    Main verb #3, subordinate verb #8:

    An sit Athēnagorās trīstis vidēbō. *I'll see whether Athenagoras is in mourning or not.* II, 6, R18.

    Main verb #5, subordinate verb #8:

    Didicī quam sīs ūtilis. *I have (now) learned how useful you are.* II, 15, R65.

---

[1] Purpose clauses generally use forms #7 and #8, since their action usually follows that of the main verb.

Inflected words: verbs

c. The #2 and #5 forms, although classified as present tense, are commonly used as narrative tenses to narrate past events.[1] When used this way, the #5 form patterns with subordinate subjunctive verbs in the past tense (#7 and #9), while the #2 form may have subordinate subjunctive verbs in either the past tense (#7 or #9) or the present tense (#8 or #10).
Main verb #5, subordinate verb #7:

Canis carnem cum ferret vīdit simulācrum suum. *When a dog was carrying some meat, he saw his reflection.* II, 8, R26.

Main verb #5, subordinate verb #9:

Hī cum cēpissent cervum vastī corporis, sīc est locūtus leō. *When they had caught a large-bodied deer, the lion spoke thus.* II, 12, R50.

Main verb #2, subordinate verb #7:

Ut idem cōnarētur persuādet. *He persuaded him to try the same thing.* II, 19, BG3.

Main verb #2, subordinate verb #10:

Crīminātur fīlium quod rem fēminārum tetigerit. *She accused the son because he touched something which belonged to women.* II, 15, R62.

---

[1] See p. 75, fn 1 and 2.

These rules may be schematized as follows:

Main clause indicative		
Past	Present	Future
#1 dūcēbās	#2 dūcis	#3 dūcēs
#4 dūxerās	#5 dūxistī	#6 dūxeris
Subordinate clause subjunctive		
Past	Present	—
#7 dūcerēs	#8 dūcās	—
#9 dūxissēs	#10 dūxerīs	—

2. Use of the subjunctive in conditions.[1] All four forms of the subjunctive are used in conditions. The following are the most common combinations:
   a. The "should, would" condition: present imperfective subjunctive (#8) is used in both clauses

   Nisī per tē <u>sapiās</u>, frūstrā sapientem <u>audiās</u>. *Unless you should be wise of your own accord, you would listen to a wise man in vain.* LS5, p. 36.

   b. Present contrary-to-fact: past imperfective subjunctive (#7) is used in both clauses to say something which would be true if something else were true (but is not).

   Sī <u>foret</u> in terrīs, <u>rīdēret</u> Dēmocritus. *If Democritus were on earth [which he is not], he would be laughing [which he is not].* II, 12, S51.

---

[1] All tenses of the indicative may also be used in conditions:
   Sī vērum <u>est</u>, <u>laudat</u> carmina nostra Mathō. *If this is [actually] so, Matho praises my poems.* II, 13, R54.
See also § 20, fn1 for the translation of the #6 tense in conditions.

Inflected words: verbs

c. Past contrary-to-fact: past perfective subjunctive (#9) is used in both clauses to say something which would have been true if something else had been true (but was not).

Sī tacuissēs, philosophus mānsissēs. *If you had kept silent [which you did not do], you would have remained a philosopher [which you did not].* II, 16, S56.

3. In mixed conditions various combinations of moods, aspects, and tenses are possible. For example, there may be an indicative in one clause and a subjunctive in the other

Simia simia est etiam sī aurea gestet īnsīgnia. *A monkey is a monkey even if he should wear golden decorations.* LS5, p. 36.

or two different subjunctive tenses in two different clauses

Illud mīrārer, sī fābulantem Canium reliquisset. *I would [now] be astonished if he had [in the past] left Canius while he was telling a story.* LS15, p. 124.

VI. *Aspect* describes the nature of the action of the verb. See § 20.

A. The imperfective aspect indicates an ongoing (incomplete) action

#1 **Langūēbam.** *I was lying in bed sick.* I, 28, R2.
#2 **Laudat, amat, cantat, nostrōs mea Rōma libellōs.** *My Rome is [now] praising, loving, and reciting my books.* I, 29, R5[1].
#3 **Formōsus septem, Mārce, diēbus eris.** *Marcus, you will be handsome in seven days.* I, 28, R1.

B. The perfective aspect indicates a completed action

#4 **Quod vespillo facit, fēcerat et medicus.** *What he does now as an undertaker, he had done also as a doctor.* I, 28, R3.
#5 **Bonum certāmen certāvī, cursum cōnsummāvī, fidem servāvī.** *I have fought the good fight, I have finished the race, I have kept the faith.* I, 27, S129[2].
#6 **Citō rumpēs arcum, semper sī tēnsum habueris.** *You will quickly break your bow, if you always keep [will have kept] it stretched.* I, 29, S141.

---

[1] The #2 tense is also used as a narrative tense. It presents past action as if it were going on at the present time and thus carries an overtone of vividness.
[2] The #5 tense is most commonly used as a narrative tense. When used in this way, it describes past events *without* implying that the events are complete in the present. See § 20.

Participles

There are four verbal adjectives, or "participles," which "participate" in, or share features of, two classes of words: adjectives and verbs. Participles are like adjectives because
- they have number, gender, and case
- they may modify nouns
- some of them may take the place of nouns

They are like verbs because
- they have voice, aspect, and tense
- they may take the same complement as the verb from which they are derived

I. The imperfective active participle (the "present" participle) is used when the action it represents is *simultaneous* with that of the main verb. In the sentence

> **Canis aliam praedam ab alterō ferrī putāns, ēripere voluit.** *The dog, thinking that the other booty was being carried by another [dog], wanted to seize it.* II, 8, R26.

the dog is thinking about the booty and wanting to seize it at the same time.

II. The perfective passive participle (the "past" participle) is used when the action it represents is *completed* before the time of the main verb. In the sentence

> **Plōrātur lacrimīs āmissa pecūnia vērīs.** *Lost money is wept over by true tears.* I, 18, S60.

the money has been lost before the tears begin.

III. The future active participle is used when the action it represents will take place *after* the time of the main verb. In the sentence

> **Moritūrī tē salūtāmus!** *We who are about to die salute you!* II, 13, S52.

the gladiators salute before they die.

IV. The imperfective future passive participle (the "gerundive")

   A. With a form of the verb **sum**, it expresses the idea of "necessity."

      1. As the complement of **sum**

> **Carthāgō dēlenda est.** *Carthage must be destroyed.* II, 17, S62.

      2. As an impersonal verb

> **Dēlīberandum est saepe, statuendum est semel.** *One should deliberate often but decide just once.* II, 17, S64.

Inflected words: verbal nouns

B. As a modifier of the object of the preposition **ad**, it shows purpose. See II, p. 89.

Ad eās rēs cōnficiendās Orgetorīx dēligitur. *Orgetorix was chosen to accomplish these things [so these things would get done]*[1] II, 19, B63.

Verbal nouns

I. Infinitive

   A. Used like a noun in the nominative[2]

   1. As the subject of a few verbs, most commonly **sum** plus certain adjectives and impersonal verbs, such as **licet** and **opportet**

      Nātūram quidem mūtāre difficile est. *It is difficult to change Nature, anyway.* I, 24, S100.
      Nōn licet in bello bis peccāre. *To make a mistake twice is not permitted in war.* II, 19, S75.

   2. Rarely, as a complement in an [-s -s -est] construction

      Ōrāre est labōrāre. *To pray is to work.* or *To work is to pray.* LP24, p. 143.

   3. As a historical infinitive: it presents the verb without signals for person, number, tense, or mood, but with signals for voice (active or passive) and aspect (imperfective only)

      Diem ex diē dūcere Aeduī. *The Aeduans led [Caesar] on day after day.* II, 23, BG16.

   B. Used like a noun in the accusative as the object of some transitive verbs[3]

      Animum dēbēs mūtāre. *You ought to change your attitude.* I, 24, S104.

   C. Patterns with the adjectives **potis** and **parātus**

      mordēre parātī, *prepared to bite* LS1, p. 8.

---

[1] Or, more literally, *Orgetorix was chosen for these must-be-done things.*
[2] The infinitive itself is not declined for case.
[3] Among the verbs which take the infinitive as object are

coepī	īgnōrō	moneō	poscō	vetō
cupiō	incipiō	nesciō	quaerō
dēsinō	jubeō	nōscō	sciō

Most numerous are the **verba sentiendī.**

D. Used as the complement of a few intransitive verbs: cōnsuēscō, nequeō, possum, soleō

> **Levis est dolar quī capere cōnsilium potest.** *The grief which can make a plan is light.* I, 25, S110.

E. Used in a citation. The infinitive form is frequently used to cite a verb[1]

> **"Rubēre" est verbum intransitīvum.** *"Rubēre" is an intransitive verb.*

F. Used as a verb in indirect statement[2]

1. The imperfective infinitive is used when the action it represents does not occur before that of the main verb. In the sentence

   > **Tē crēdō surripere quod pulchrē negās.** *I believe that you are stealing what you cleverly deny.*

   the stealing (**surripere**) is going on at the same time the writer is expressing his opinion about it (**crēdō**).

2. The perfective infinitive is used when the action it represents occurs before that of the main verb. In the sentence

   > **Tē crēdō surripuisse quod pulchrē negās.** *I believe that you have stolen what you cleverly deny.* II, 13, R55.

   the stealing (**surripuisse**) has been completed before the writer expresses his opinion (**crēdō**).

3. The future active infinitive (expressed in the form of a participle with or without **esse**) is used when the action it represents occurs after the main verb

   > **Allobrogibus sēsē persuāsūrōs existimābant.** *They thought that they would persuade the Allobrogians.* II, 20, BG6.

4. The future passive infinitive is rarely used.

---

[1] The 1st person sg of the #2 form of the verb is also used as a citation form: **nesciō**.
[2] See discussion of indirect statement on pp. 90-91.

II. Gerund

    A. Used in the accusative as the object of a preposition, generally **ad**

> **Breve tempus aetātis; satis est longum ad bene honestēque vivendum.** *The time of life is short; it is long enough for living virtuously and honorably.* II, 18, S71.

    B. Used in the ablative, usually without a preposition, to modify the verb

> **Dēlīberandō discitur sapientia.** *Wisdom is learned by deliberation.* II, 18, S67.

    C. Used only rarely in the dative with adjectives like **aptus** and **idōneus**; this use does not occur in *Artēs Latīnae*.

    D. Used in the genitive to modify nouns

> **Legendi semper occāsiō est, audiendi nōn semper.** *There is always an opportunity for reading, there is not always an opportunity for listening.* II, 18, S70.

III. Supine

    A. Used in the accusative only after verbs of motion, without any preposition and only in short phrases

> **Spectātum veniunt.** *They come to see.* II, 21, S79.

    B. Occurs in the ablative only with a few verbs and coupled with only a few adjectives. These combinations are so rare that they are almost formulas

> **perfacile factū esse,** *to be easy to do* II, 19, BG3.

SYNTAX OF NONINFLECTED WORDS

Ten parts of speech in Latin are not inflected: coordinating conjunctions, subordinating conjunctions, sentence connectors, interjections, intensifiers, prepositions, qualifiers, noun substitutors, adjectivals, and adverbs.

    I. Coordinating conjunctions (**atque, aut, neque, et**; see Morphology, p. 30)

        A. They connect words or constructions that fill the same slot. In the sentence

> **Multae rēgum aurēs atque oculī.** *Many are the ears and eyes of kings.* I, 23, S95.

aures and **oculi** are nouns filling the same slot in an [-s -s -est] sentence. Generally the words connected by a coordinating conjunction are in the same case. However, sometimes variant constructions that fill the same slot may be connected by a coordinating conjunction.[1] In the clause

> **cum in opere et arāns esse inventus**, *when he was discovered at work and plowing* LS15, p. 121.

in opere and **arāns** are connected, even though **arāns** is a participle (in the nominative) and **in opere** is a prepositional phrase (in the ablative).

B. They are regularly found between the two structures they connect [2]

> **Semper agis causās et rēs agis, Attale, semper.** *You are always pleading lawsuits, Attalus, and you are always engaging in business.* II, 5, R14.

Here **et** comes between the two clauses it is connecting. Occasionally, words are put in front of the coordinating conjunction for emphasis

> **Tempora mūtantur, nōs et mūtāmur in illīs.** *Times change and we change with them.* II, 10, S44.

II. Subordinating conjunctions (**cum, nē, sicut**; see Morphology, p. 30)

A. They introduce a "subordinate" clause and attach it to a "main" clause. The subordinate clause serves to explain or qualify the main clause.

1. Some, like **quamvīs, licet,** and **nē,** pattern with the subjunctive only

> **Attale, nē quod agās dēsit, agās animam.** *Attalus, so that there won't be anything lacking for you to do, you should drop dead.* II, 5, R14.

2. Others, like **cum** and **ut,** pattern with either the indicative or subjunctive, depending on the meaning. In the sentence

> **Mulier, cum sōla cōgitat, male cōgitat.** *Whenever a woman thinks alone, she thinks badly.* I, 19, S64.

the use of the indicative shows that **cum** means "whenever." In contrast, when **cum**

---

[1] See the discussion of variant constructions on pp. 40-41.
[2] Except **-que**, which is attached to the second of the two words it connects.
   Senātus Populusque Rōmānus. *The Senate and the Roman people* LP1, p. 1.

Noninflected words: sentence connectors

means *when, because, since,* or *although,* the verb occurs in the subjunctive. In the sentence

Nīl bene cum faciās, faciās tamen omnia bellē. *Although you do nothing well, still you do everything cleverly.*

The presence of **tamen,** *however,* indicates that, in this subordinate subjunctive clause, **cum** means *although.*

B. They regularly are the first word in their clause

Cum corvus cāseum comēsse vellet, vulpēs invīdit. *When a crow wanted to eat up some cheese, a fox envied him.* II, 12, R49.

Modification: for emphasis, one or more words may be placed in front of the subordinating conjunction

canis per flūmen carnem cum ferret natāns, *when a dog was carrying some meat, while swimming through a river* II, 8, R26.

III. Sentence connectors (**at, igitur, nam;** see p. 30).

A. They connect the sentence with the preceding sentence. Thus they can never be part of an opening sentence [1]

Nōn faciam. Nam vīs vendere, nōn legere. *I won't do it. For you want to sell them, not read them.* II, 5, R11.

B. They regularly are among the first four words in their clause.

1. Some, like **nam** and **vērum,** almost always are the first word in their clause

Vērum perītīs irritōs tendit dolōs. *But he stretches his snares in vain for experienced people.* II, 14, R58.

2. Some, such as **enim** and **autem,** are almost never the first word in the clause

Frīgus enim magnum synthesis ūna facit. *For my one set of clothes keeps me very cool (makes for great coolness).* II, 16, R71.

---

[1] The opening line of *Guadeāmus Igitur* is no exception since it is traditionally sung at the end of a songfest. The purpose of the **igitur** is to link all of the songs together.

IV. Interjections (ēn, ecce, heus; see p. 30). Interjections indicate the speaker's emotions. Unlike most Latin words, they do not fill any particular slot in the sentence and can be introduced by the speaker at any point[1] without changing the structure of the sentence

>Mortis ēn sōlācium! *Look! A consolation for death.* II, 7, R25.
>Pater, Hercle, tuus male dīxit mihī. *Your father, by Hercules, cursed me.* II, 11, R47.

V. Intensifiers, negators, and interrogators. These are classed together on the basis of syntactic similarity, but they have distinct uses in the Latin sentence.

  A. Uses

   1. Intensifiers (**etiam, modo, quidem, ūsque**; see p. 31). These emphasize a word, phrase, clause, or sentence

    >Nātūram quidem mūtāre difficile est. *It is difficult to change Nature, anyway.* I, 24, S100.

   2. Negators (**nōn, haud**; see p. 31). These single out a word, phrase, clause, or sentence and negate it

    >Aquila nōn capit muscās. *An eagle does not catch flies.* I, 14, S36.

   3. Interrogators (**an, -ne**, see p. 31) turn a statement into a question

    >Adeōne pulchra est? *Is she all that pretty?* II, 9, R31.

  B. Position in Latin sentence

   1. Intensifiers and negators occur next to the item they intensify or negate.[2]
      a. Some, such as **et, etiam**, and all negators, regularly precede the word they modify

      >Impōnit fīnem sapiēns et rēbus honestīs. *The wise person puts a limit to even honorable endeavors.* I, 21, S78.

      b. Some, such as **quoque**, follow the word they intensify

      >Rōmae quoque hominēs moriuntur. *Men die also at Rome.* LS10, p. 74.

   2. Interrogators appear regularly as the first word (or attached to the first word) of the sentence or main clause.

---

[1] **Heus**, however, comes first in its clause; it calls attention to the entire utterance to follow.
[2] See p. 88.

VI. Prepositions (see p. 31.)

   A. They take (or "govern") a noun in either the accusative or ablative case;[1] the resulting "prepositional phrase" usually modifies the verb in the sentence of which it is a part. In the sentence

> **Stultum est querī dē adversīs ubi culpa est tua.** *It is stupid to complain about difficulties when the fault is your own.* II, 3, S19.

the prepositional phrase **de adversīs** modifies the verb **querī**, telling what it is stupid to complain about. A few prepositions, such as **in**, are often omitted, particularly in poetry.[2]

   B. They generally are placed before the noun they pattern with

> **Jam ego ūnō in saltū lepidē aprōs capiam duōs.** *Now I will cleverly capture two boars in one jump.* I, 26, S121.

However, they may come before a modifier of the noun they govern

> **Nōs beātam vītam in animī sēcūritāte pōnimus.** *We believe that a happy life lies in security of mind.* I, 25, S108.

Exceptions:

1. Two-syllable prepositions, such **infrā**, sometimes follow the noun they govern

> **Rēgna īnfrā caelī quiēscō.** *I lie below the realms of the sky.* LP26, p. 164.

2. The preposition **cum** always follows and becomes joined to personal pronouns

> **mēcum**   not   *cum mē

and often behaves in the same way with the interrogative or relative pronoun, as in

> **quōcum**

---

[1] See p. 31 for prepositions that take the acc and pp. 31 and 32 for those that take the abl. Of the prepositions in *Artēs Latīnae,* only **in** and **sub** can take either abl or acc, the abl showing *where?* and the acc showing *into where?*
> **Mēns sāna in corpore sānō.** *A sound mind in a sound body.* I, 13, S30.
> **Cum dēcidisset vulpēs in puteum.** *When a fox had fallen into a well.* II, 12, R51.

[2] See b, p. 47 for omission of prepositions with the abl.

VII. Qualifiers (**tam, nimis, vix**; see Morphology, p. 32). Qualifiers modify verbs, adjectives, and adverbs by telling *How much?* (**Quam?**) They are generally placed next to the word they qualify

>**Nōn faciam tam fatuē.** *I won't act so stupidly.* II, 5, R13.
>**Adeōne pulchra est?** *Is she so beautiful?* II, 9, R31.

Some words used as adverbs are also used as qualifiers

>**Bene celeriter currit.** *He runs quite quickly.*

VIII. Noun substitutors (**adhūc, mox, ōlim, posteā**; see Morphology, p. 32 and § 11), as the name suggests, substitute for noun phrases of the same meaning. Like noun phrases, they usually modify the verb

>**grandis ut exiguam bōs rānam rūperat ōlim,** *as the huge cow once broke the tiny frog* II, 9, R29.

IX. Adverbs (see Morphology, p. 34)

A. Adverbs modify verbs.

1. Most adverbs answer the question *In what way?* (**Qualiter?**)

   >**Inopī beneficium bis dat quī dat celeriter.** *He who gives quickly to a poor man gives the benefit twice.* I, 20, S70.

2. Some adverbs (particularly those in -**im**) may answer other questions, such as *When?* (**Quandō?**)

   >**Interim cottidiē Caesar Aeduōs frūmentum flāgitāre.** *In the meantime, Caesar demanded the grain from the Aeduans.* II, 23, BG16.

3. Adverbial numerals and a few adverbs not formed on a noun, adjective, or verb base, such as **semel** and **bis**, answer the question *How often?* (**Quotiēns?**)

   >**Ūndeciēns ūnā surrēx'tī, Zōile, cēnā.** *Zoilus, you got up eleven times in one meal.* II, 16, R71.

B. They are generally placed near the noun they modify.

Noninflected words: adjectivals

X. Adjectivals (**quattuor, satis**; see Morphology, p. 35)

  A. They may replace an adjective without changing the structure of the sentence. Since in this way they fill the slot of an adjective, they are called adjectivals. They are not true adjectives, however, since they are not inflected for gender, number, or case. In the sentence

  Castaneās centum sēvit Otācilius. *Otacilius planted a hundred chestnuts.* II, 9, R29.

  the adjectival **centum** modifies **castaneās**.

  B. To avoid ambiguity, adjectivals usually come near the noun they modify.

Part III
Selected topics in Latin sentence construction

WORD ORDER

I. General rule: Latin word order is free within each clause

> **Religiō deōs colit, superstitiō violat.** *Religion honors the gods, superstition violates them.* I, 14, S37.

means the same thing as

> **Colit deōs religiō, violat superstitiō.**

and the same thing as

> **Deōs colit religiō, superstitiō violat.**

and so on.[1]

II. There are, however, certain common word orders.

   A. The "normal order," that is, the most common order, of a sentence is subject, complement, verb

> **Vestis virum reddit.** *Clothes make the man.* I, 2, S1.

---

[1] But words from different clauses cannot be interchanged: the word order
    Superstitiō deōs colit, religiō violat. *Superstition honors the gods, religion violates them.*
completely changes the meaning of the sentence.

B. Adjectives and genitives are usually found next to (more often following) the noun they modify

> **Amicus certus in rē incertā cernitur.** *A sure friend is discovered in an unsure situation.* I, 11, S24.
>
> **quod rem fēminārum tetegerit,** *because he had touched something [belonging to] women* II, 15, R62.

Modifications:

1. Demonstrative and intensive pronominal adjectives, cardinal numbers, and adjectives of quantity generally precede the nouns they modify

   > **Lis est dē tribus capellīs.** *The lawsuit is about three little goats.* II, 11, R45.

2. When an adjective is separated from the noun it modifies, both it and the noun are greatly emphasized. In the clause

   > **Homō in peric'lum simul ac vēnit callidus,** *as soon as a clever man gets into danger* II, 12, R51.

   both the adjective, **callidus**, and the noun it modifies, **homō**, are emphasized by the device of separating them.

3. In poetry, rhyming nouns and adjectives are frequently separated, thus receiving emphasis both from the rhyme and from their separated position. **Oculō** and **alterō** are treated in this way in the line

   > **Oculō Philaenis semper alterō plōrat.** *Philaenis always weeps with one eye.* II, 6, R20.

C. Certain parts of speech, such as subordinating conjunctions, are regularly the first word in their clause.

Modification: other words may precede the subordinating conjunction or relative pronoun introducing their clause in order to receive emphasis. In the clause

> **casta suō gladium cum trāderet Arria Paetō,** *when virtuous Arria gave the sword to her own Paetus* II, 9, R34.

the words *virtuous* (**casta**), *her own* (**suō**), and *sword* (**gladium**) are given great emphasis by their position, before **cum**.

D. **Sī** and **cum** clauses regularly precede the main clause

> **Sī rēs et causae dēsunt, agis, Attale, mūlās.** *If there are no business affairs or lawsuits, Attalus, you drive mules.* II, 5, R14.

E. Intensifiers, negators, and qualifiers regularly precede the word, phrase, clause, or sentence they modify. Two exceptions are **quidem** and **quoque**, which follow the words they modify.[1]

F. In a series, 1st person pronouns (**egō** and **nōs**) regularly precede those of the 2d person (**tū** and **vōs**) and those of the 2d person regularly precede those of the 3d

> **Nē <u>mihi tū</u> mittās, Pontiliāne, tuōs.** *So that you won't send me yours, Pontilianus.* II, 5, R10.

III. There are a very few instances where word order is not free.

A. Negators precede the word or words they negate. If the entire sentence is negated, the negator precedes the verb; for emphasis the negator may precede the entire sentence. In the sentences

> **<u>Nōn omnēs</u> eadem mīrantur amantque.** *Not all people admire and like the same things.* II, 1, S4.
> **<u>Nōn quaerit</u> aeger medicum ēloquentem.** *A sick person doesn't seek a talkative doctor.* I, 6, S9.

omnēs and **quaerit** are negated.

Exception:

In a few cases, changed word order changes the meaning

nōn nūllus, *someone*	**nōn numquam,** *sometimes*	**nōn nihil,** *something*
nūllus nōn, *everyone*	**numquam nōn,** *always*	**nihil nōn,** *everything*

B. Certain phrases, such as **rēs pūblica** and **populus Rōmānus**, occur in a fixed order.

C. Certain noninflected words, such as **enim, autem, quoque,** and **quidem,** rarely or never begin a sentence. The verb **inquit** never begins a direct quotation but must follow at least one word of it.

---

[1] See V B b , p. 82 and III C , this page.

EXPRESSION OF PURPOSE

In *Artēs Latīnae,* purpose is expressed in four ways.

I. The most common way is **ut** (negative, **nē**) with the subjunctive

> **Vēnit ut cēnāret.** *He came so that he might dine.*
> **Vēnit nē cēnāret.** *He came so that he might not dine.*

Variations:

A. The **ut** clause may sometimes be replaced by a relative clause

> **Mīsit amīcōs quī cēnārent.** *He sent friends who were to dine.*

B. The **ut** is replaced by **quō** when the subordinate clause it introduces contains a comparative

> **Vēnit quō celerius cēnāret.** *He came in order to dine more quickly.*

II. Purpose may also be expressed by **ad** with a gerund

> **Vēnit ad cēnandum.** *He came for the purpose of dining.*

Variation: When the gerund takes an object, as in

> **Vēnit ad cōnficiendum eās rēs.** *He came to accomplish these things.*

the following construction is more common: the object of the gerund (here **eās rēs**) can be made the object of the preposition **ad**, modified by the gerundive. See IV B, p. 77.

> **Vēnit ad eās rēs cōnficiendās.** *He came to accomplish these things. [He came for these to-be-accomplished things.]*

III. A less common construction is **causā** with the gerund or gerundive in the genitive case. In the sentence

> **Caesar nāvium parandārum causā morātur.** *Caesar delays to prepare the ships [for the sake of the ships which had to be prepared].* LS 24, p. 241.

causā is used with the gerundive. The sentence

> **Caesar nāvis parandī causā morātur.** *Caesar delays to prepare the ships [for the sake of preparing the ships].*

uses **causā** and the gerund in *Artēs Latīnae* to express the same idea.

IV. The least common construction is the supine in **-um**

> **Vēnit cēnātum.** *He came to dine.*

It is regularly used in short expressions and only after verbs of motion.

INDIRECT DISCOURSE

I. Indirect statement

A. Formed from a direct statement by adding a suitable **verbum sentiendī** (symbol {VS}) or using one already contained in the direct statement, changing the subject of the direct statement to the accusative case (symbol {-m}), and transforming the finite verb to the infinitive (symbol {-re}).
Direct statement: **"Mārcus cēnat."** *"Marcus is dining."*
Indirect statement: **Titus dīcit Mārcum cēnāre.** *Titus says that Marcus is dining.*
Formula: {VS} {-m} {-re} .

B. Expression of tense

1. The imperfective infinitive is used when the action of the indirect statement is happening at the same time the report is made

> **Titus dīcit Mārcum cēnāre.** *Titus says that Marcus is [now] dining.*
> **Titus dīxit Mārcum cēnāre.** *Titus said that Marcus was dining [at that time].*

2. The perfective infinitive is used when the action took place before the report was made

> **Titus dīcit Mārcum cēnāvisse.** *Titus says that Marcus dined.*
> **Titus dīxit Mārcum cēnāvisse.** *Titus said that Marcus had dined.*

Indirect discourse

3. The future participle with esse[1] (the future active infinitive) is used when the action will take place after the report is made

   Titus dīcit Mārcum cēnātūrum esse. *Titus says that Marcus will dine.*
   Titus dīxit Mārcum cēnātūrum esse. *Titus said that Marcus would dine.*

4. The future passive infinitive is rarely used.

C. Subordinate clauses in indirect statement: all subordinate verbs become subjunctive. If, in an indirect statement, a verb in a subordinate clause is not in the subjunctive, this clause is not part of the reported statement but a parenthetical insert by someone else.[2]

Direct statement: **Titus ait: "Mārcus, quī semper hilaris est, cēnat."** *Titus says, "Marcus, who is always cheerful, is dining."*
Indirect statement: **Titus dīcit Mārcum, quī semper hilaris sit, cēnāre.** *Titus says that Marcus, who [Titus says] is always cheerful, is dining.*

This contrasts with the use of the indicative in the subordinate clause

   Titus dīcit Mārcum, quī semper hilaris est, cēnāre. *Titus says that Marcus* (Editor's note: *Marcus is always cheerful) is dining.*

II. Indirect question: formed from a direct question by using the same question word (symbol {qu-}), adding a suitable **verbum sentiendī** (symbol {VS}) or using the one from the direct question and transforming the verb of the direct question to the subjunctive (symbol {-ā-}).[3]

Direct question: **"Cūr Mārcus cēnat?"** *"Why is Marcus dining?"*
Indirect question: **Titus quaerit cūr Mārcus cēnet.** *Titus asks why Marcus is dining.*

Formula: {VS} {qu-} {-ā-} .

III. Indirect commands. There are two ways to form an indirect command from a direct command, depending on the **verbum sentiendī** chosen to report it.

   A. With certain **verba sentiendī**, such as **dīcō** and **imperō** (symbol {VS}), indirect command is formed by adding {ut} (or {nē}), transforming the vocative (if any) to a dative, and putting the verb of the direct command into the subjunctive (symbol {-ā-}).

---

[1] The verb **esse** is often omitted.
[2] See e., pp. p. 71.
[3] The rules of sequence of tenses apply. See B. 1, pp. 72-74.

Direct command: **"Mārce, cēnā!"** *"Marcus, dine!"*
Indirect command: **Titus Mārcō dīcit ut cēnet.** *Titus tells Marcus to dine [that he should dine].*

Formula: $\{VS\}\{ut\}\{-ā-\}$.

B. With some other **verba sentiendī**, such as **jubeō** (symbol $\{VS\}$), indirect command is formed by changing the vocative to the accusative (symbol $\{-m\}$) and transforming the verb of the direct command to the infinitive (symbol $\{-re\}$).

Direct command: **"Mārce, cēnā!"** *"Marcus, dine!"*
Indirect command: **Titus Mārcum cēnāre jubet.** *Titus orders Marcus to dine.*

Formula: $\{VS\}\{-m\}\{-re\}$.

EXPRESSION OF DIRECT COMMAND

I. There are four ways to form a direct command:

A. By using the first imperative

> **Dīc, Postume, dē tribus capellīs.** *Speak, Postumus, about the three goats.* II, 11, R45.

B. (More politely) by using the subjunctive

> **Dīcās, Postume, dē tribus capellīs.** *Postumus, I would like you to speak about the three goats.*

C. (Most politely) by using the imperfective future (#3) tense

> **Dīcēs, Postume, dē tribus capellīs.** *You will, Postumus, [I hope] speak about the three goats.*

D. By using the second imperative (see § 11). This form is generally used in formal language, like laws and prayers, and in informal language, like personal letters

> **Dīcitō, Postume, dē tribus capellīs.** *Speak, Postumus, about the three goats.*

Expression of direct command

II. There are two standard ways to express negative command, although the subjunctive and the imperfective future tense may also be used as in positive command.

   A. By using **nōlī** (or **nōlīte**) plus the infinitive

   Nōlī dē tribus capellīs, Postume, dīcere. *Do not speak about the three goats, Postumus.*

   B. (More strongly) by using a negative word, such as **ne** or **nihil**, with the present perfective subjunctive (#10) form of the verb

   Nihil abritriō vīrium fēceris. *Do nothing at the dictate of violence.* LS15, p. 125.

Advanced notes

§ 1 **Regular vowel and consonant changes** [p. 2] [1]

Morphology includes an analysis of how vowels and consonants change in different forms of a word. Knowledge of regular changes will allow you to recognize some unfamiliar words as derived from words you already know. The following are some of the more common regular changes:

    a. Vowel weakening. When a word is compounded, the vowel of the stem often changes. The most common changes are **a → i**, **ae → ī**, and **e → i**.

        ē+rapere → ēripere
        in+amīcus → inimīcus
        re+quaerere → requīrere
        in+aequus → inīquus
        con+legō → colligō

    b. Vowel shortening.

       1. A long vowel becomes short before another vowel[2]

          veniat   not   *****veniāt**

       2. A long vowel becomes short before final -t, final -m, and final -r[3]

          invenit   not   *****invenīt**
          inveniēbam   not   *****inveniēbām**
          inveniar   not   *****inveniār**

---

[1] Page numbers in brackets refer back to the page in the text on which the *Note* is first cited.
[2] **Fīō** and **diēī** are exceptions, as are some Greek nouns, such as **Aenēās** and **Thāida**.
[3] In poetry, the long vowel is occasionally retained, as in **Omnia vincit Amōr.** *Love conquers all.* II, 4, S25.

Defective nouns

3. A long vowel becomes short before medial or final -nt

> amant   not   *amānt
> amantur   not   amāntur

c. Assimilation. The last consonant of a prefix frequently becomes the same as the first consonant of the verb stem.[1]

> ad+capere → accipere   not   *adcipere
> ex+fugere → effugere   not   *exfugere

§ 2 The locative case

The locative case has the signal -ī. It occurs only in a few words, which are the names of towns, cities, and small islands, and in the words **domus** and **rūs**.

nominative	locative
bellus	bellī, *in war*
domus	domī, *at home*
humus	humī, *on the ground*
mīlitia	mīlitiae,[2] *in the battlefield*
Rōma	Rōmae,[2] *at Rome*
rūs	rūrī, *in the country*
vesperus	vesperī, *in the evening*

§ 3 Defective nouns

Some nouns do not have all ten possible forms. Examples are
  a. Nouns with only one form, such as

> cottīdiē, *every day*
> noctū, *at night*
> postrīdiē, *on the next day*
> [suā] sponte, *of [his own] desire*

  b. Nouns with only two forms, such as

> nom fors   ⎫
> abl forte ⎬ *chance*

---

[1] Some words have both assimilated and unassimilated variant forms:
    sub+primō → supprimō   and   subprimō

[2] -ī added to -a is written -ae.

c. At the other extreme are nouns with only one form missing. The following are the genitive forms of three common nouns which are lacking the nominative singular form:

> opis,[1] *aid*
> dapis, *feast*
> vicis, *change*

§ 4 Variant nouns of the 2d declension [p. 4]

A small subclass consists of three neuter nouns, two of which occur in *Artēs Latīnae*. They are declined like **rēgnum** except that the nominative and accusative singular both end in -s:

sg	pl	sg	pl
vulgus	vulga	pelagus	pelega
vulgus	vulga	pelagus	pelaga
vulgō	vulgnīs	pelagō	pelagīs
vulgō	vulgnīs	pelagō	pelagīs
vulgī	vulgnōrum	pelagī	pelagōrum

§ 5 Variant nouns of the 3d declension [p. 5]

A small subclass has -i- in all forms of the singular. Examples in *Artēs Latīnae* are **sitis, febris, puppis,** and **tussis**.

sg   (pl is regular)

puppis
puppim
puppī
puppī
puppis

§ 6 Greek noun forms [p. 6]

Artēs Latīnae readings contain a few Greek nouns whose forms are different from Latin nouns. For example the nominative singular form **Lycōris** has the accusative singular form **Lycōrida**. The following Greek forms occur in the programmed text:

> **Aeacidā**, voc sg
> **Hectora**, acc sg
> **Lingonas**, acc pl
> **Thāida**, acc sg

---

[1] Words like **ops** are nom forms constructed for listing in dictionaries and grammars.

3d declension adjectives

Examples of Greek forms in *Lēctiōnēs Secundae* include:[1]

nom sg in -ē	*nom sg in -s*	*acc sg in -n*	*acc sg in -a*
Amynonē	Dēlos	Amīson	āera
Berenīcē	melos	Commāgēnēn	aethera
Cyrēnē	Prūsiās	Cotyn	Baucida
Īrēnē	scorpios	Mithridātēn	Chalcēdona
Phoenīcē		Nisibin	crātēra
Sophranēnē		Orodēn	diadēma
Zōē		Sinōpēn	Epimēthida
		Syēnēn	Lycōrida
		Themin	Philēmona
			Trītōna

gen sg	*voc sg*	*nom pl*	*acc pl*	*gen pl*
Cyanēs	Themi	Charites	Cōrycidas	epigrammatōn
grammaticēs		Coricydes	Sīrēnas	
Libyēs		Dropes		
Persephonēs		Nēreides		
Phoenīcēs		Plejades		
Syēnēs		Sīrēnes		

§ 7 3d declension adjectives [p. 7]

3d declension adjectives can be classified by the number of forms they have in the nominative singular. A "one ending" adjective has only one form for all three genders in the nominative singular; examples are **fēlix** and all present participles, such as **vocāns**. A "two ending" adjective has one form for masculine and feminine and one nominative singular form for neuter, such as **facilis, facile**. A "three ending" adjective has separate forms for each gender in the nominative singular, such as **ācer, ācris, ācre**.

---

[1] These forms are grouped here only by surface resemblance, not by Greek decl.

One ending adjective of 3d declension

Singular

m & f	n
fēlīx	fēlīx
fēlīcem	fēlīx
fēlīcī, -e[1]	fēlīcī, -e[1]
fēlīcī	fēlīcī
fēlīcis	fēlīcis

Plural

m & f	n
fēlīcēs	fēlīcia
fēlīcēs	fēlīcia
fēlīcibus	fēlīcibus
fēlīcibus	fēlīcibus
fēlīcium	fēlīcium

Three ending adjectives of 3d declension

Singular

m	f	n
ācer	ācris	ācre
ācrem	ācrem	ācre
ācrī	ācrī	ācrī
ācrī	ācrī	ācrī
ācris	ācris	ācris

Plural

m	f	n
ācrēs	ācrēs	ācria
ācrēs, -īs	ācrēs, -īs	ācria
ācribus	ācribus	ācribus
ācribus	ācribus	ācribus
ācrium	ācrium	ācrium

§ 8 **Characteristic vowels of verbs** [p. 14]

The characteristic vowels given are determined from the infinitive form. However, these vowels do not always predominate throughout the paradigm of the verb. For example, the characteristic vowel is often ∅ in the perfective system of the 2d conjugation, as in **mōv+∅+ī** and in the imperfective system of the 3d conjugation, as in **ag+∅+ēs**.

The 3d conjugation presents a further complication, because although the characteristic vowel of the infinitive is -e-, the characteristic vowels ∅ and -i- (as in **ag+i+s**) actually predominate in the paradigm. Thus we may say that the 3d conjugation has three characteristic vowels: -e-, ∅, and -i-.

Verbs of the 3d conjugation in -iō, such as **capiō**, have these same three characteristic vowels. An -i- is attached to the lexical stem when the vowel is ∅: **cap+i+∅+ēbam** (compared with **ag+∅+ēbam**). When the characteristic vowel is -i- or -e-, the additional -i- does not appear, as in **cap+i+s** (compared with **ag+i+s**).

---

[1] The form fēlīcī is more common than fēlīce.

§9 Formation of perfective verbs [p. 15]

While it is true that the perfective active stem is not predictable, nevertheless it is generally formed in one of five ways:

a. By adding the characteristic vowel and the letter -v- to the lexical stem

> **laudō, laudāre, laudāvī, laudātus**
> **audiō, audīre, audīvī, audītus**

This pattern is found with most (but not all) 1st and 4th conjugation verbs.

b. By adding -u- to the lexical stem

> **habeō, habēre, habuī, habitus**
> **aperiō, aperīre, aperuī, apertus**

c. By adding -s- to the lexical stem

> **maneō, manēre, mānsī**

Note that when -s- is added to a stem ending in -c or -g, the combined sound is written -x-

> **dūcō, dūcere, dūxī, ductus**
> **regō, regere, rēxī, rēctus**

d. By changing the vowel of the lexical stem

> **videō, vidēre, vīdī, vīsus**[1]
> **faciō, facere, fēcī, factus**

e. By prefixing another syllable beginning with the initial consonant (or consonants) of the stem

> **currō, currere, cucurrī**
> **stō, stāre, stetī**

§10 Intransitive verbs [p. 15]

Intransitive verbs do not normally have passive forms and therefore cannot use the perfective passive participle as a 4th principal part. However, some intransitive verbs may be used in the 3d person singular in an "impersonal passive" construction.[2] The neuter singular form of the

---

[1] Here the vowel change is from short -i- to long -ī-.
[2] See p. 65.

perfective impersonal passive is sometimes listed as the 4th principal part of such a verb: thus the 4th principal part of **pūgnō** is sometimes gives as **pūgnātum**, the neuter singular for the impersonal form **pūgnātum est**.[1]

Intransitive verbs that do not have an impersonal passive are sometimes listed with the future active participle as the 4th principal part, such as **maneō, manēre, mānsī, mānsūrus**.

Some transitive verbs also lack a perfective passive participle. Among those occurring in *Artēs Latīnae* are **bibō** (the form **bibitus** is extremely rare), **canō, compescō, discō, meminī, ōdī, teneō, timeō**, and **urgeō**.

§ 11 **Second imperative** [p. 19]

Forms like **laudā** are the first imperative. There is also a second imperative form, which appears in LS17. The signal for the singular of this form is **-tō**, as in **docetō**; the plural, **-tōte**, as in **docētōte**, does not occur in *Artēs Latīnae*. For the syntax of the second imperative, see p. 92.

§ 12 **Noun substitutors** [p. 32]

A noun substitutor
  a. Does not change form.
  b. Does not have any readily identifiable part that might mark it as a defective noun. **Hodiē, cottidiē**, and **postridiē** are classed as defective nouns because they are derived from **diē**, the stem of the inflected noun **diēs**, *day*.
  c. Fills the slot of a common noun phrase with little change in meaning. In

> **Nōmina stultōrum scrībuntur ubīque locōrum.** *The names of stupid people are written everywhere.* LS8, p. 55.

ubīque may be replaced by the noun phrase **omnibus in locīs**, giving

> **Nōmina stultōrum scrībuntur omnibus in locīs locōrum.**

§ 13 **Differences between English and Latin number**

  a. Most nouns in the 5th declension (excepting only **rēs** and **diēs**) have no plural, whereas their English equivalents usually do have plurals.
  b. Some nouns do not have, or rarely use, the singular, whereas their English equivalents are usually singular

> **dēliciae**, *darling*
> **nūptiae**, *marriage*

---

[1] This form may alternatively be understood as the supine.

c. In poetry the plural (particularly of neuter nouns) is sometimes used where the meaning is singular, such as **colla** (in place of **collum**), neck. LS9, p. 65.
d. Some Latin nouns are used in the singular where equivalent English nouns are used only in the plural

> **Vestis bella est.** *The clothes are beautiful.*

e. Two singular nouns joined by the conjunction **et** or **-que** frequently take a singular verb. In the sentence

> **Aequālēs scrībit librōs Calvīnus et Umber.** *Calvinus writes even books and Umber does [too].* II, 13, R54.

scrībit with its object is understood to be used twice, once with **Calvīnus** and once with **Umber** (with the second **aequālēs librōs scrībit** then deleted).

§ 14 Locative and vocative cases [p. 43]

The locative and vocative cases are different from the other cases because
a. Their forms are usually identical with another case in the paradigm, except for 2d declension vocatives (such as **Mārce** and **Sabidī**) and a few locative forms, (such as **domī**). For this reason, Latin is usually said to have five cases, not seven.
b. They have only one use in the sentence.
c. They may not be the complement of a verb.

§ 15 Transitive verbs[1] [p. 64]

a. A transitive verb is one which may be transformed from the active to the passive voice. The sentence

> **Diem nox premit.** *Night pursues day.* I, 8, S16.

may be transformed to

> **Diēs nocte premitur.** *Day is pursued by night.*

---

[1] See p. 64 for transitival verbs.

When the subject of the active verb is a personal noun, as in

> **Canis aprum tenet.** *A dog holds a boar.*

it is transformed to the ablative with **ā/ab** when the verb is transformed to the passive

> **Ā cane aper tenētur.** *A boar is held by a dog.*

b. Some transitive verbs can take two objects in the accusative,[1] of which one is often personal, one nonpersonal.

> **Rogāvī philosophum sententiam.** *I asked the philosopher his opinion.*

When these verbs are transformed to the passive, the personal noun becomes the subject and the nonpersonal noun remains the object

> **Philosophus sententiam rogātus est.** *The philosopher was asked his opinion.*

The same is true when the slot of the nonpersonal noun is taken by the infinitive

> **Jubet nōs jacēre hās post terga.** *He orders us to throw these behind our backs.*

may be transformed to

> **(Nōs) jubēmur jacēre hās post terga.**

Some transitive verbs, called "factitive" because they describe an action which makes **(facit)** somebody into something, also can take two accusatives, but in this case both become nominative when the verb is transformed to the passive.

> **Vocō Mārcum patrōnum.** *I call Marcus patron.*

may be transformed to

> **Vocātur Mārcus patrōnus.** *Marcus is called patron.*

§ 16 Dates [p. 46]

Roman dates were calculated by counting back from three places in the month, the Kalends, the Ides, and the Nones. Unlike the English method of computing time, the Romans included both the day they started counting and the day they ended in their calculation.

---

[1] See p. 45, fn 1 for a list of these verbs.

Word order with genitive

The Kalends were the first day of each month. Therefore, the expression

quīntus diēs ante Kalendās Aprīlem, *five days before the Kalends of April*

is our March 28th, calculated by counting back five days from April 1st: April 1st, March 31st, 30th, 29th, 28th.

The Ides came on the 15th day of March, July, October, and May and on the 13th day of all other months. Thus

sextus diēs ante Īdūs Mārtiās, *six days before the Ides of March*

is our March 10th, calculated by counting back six days from March 15th: March 15th, 14th, 13th, 12th, 11th, 10th.

The Nones came nine days (by the Roman system of counting) before the Ides. Thus if the Ides fell on the 15th day of the month, the Nones came on the 7th day. If the Ides fell on the 13th day of the month, the Nones came on the 5th day.

§ 17 **Word order with ablative** [p. 46]

Often, only word order makes clear whether an ablative is used to modify a verb, a noun, or an adjective. In the sentence

Fronte Selium nūbilā vidēs. *You see Selius with his gloomy face.* II, 10, R36.

the author makes use of word order by inserting **Selium** in the middle of the phrase **fronte nūbilā** to show the word that **fronte nūbilā** modifies. In this way the sentence can not mean *You see Selius by means of your gloomy face.*

§ 18 **Word order with genitive** [p. 53]

Although there is no structural signal to tell which noun a genitive modifies, it generally modifies the nearest noun with which it is semantically compatible. Thus the sentence

Glōria umbra virtūtis est. I, 22, S86.

probably means *Glory is the shadow of virtue.* rather than *The glory of virtue is a shadow.*

§ 19 Subjunctive of characteristic [p. 71]

The use of the subjunctive in the clause

> [Amphora] odōrem quae jūcundum lātē spargeret

is a subtle one. In translation the clause would probably be rendered the same way if the indicative were used

> **Amphora odōrem quae jūcundum lātē spargēbat,** *a jar which gave off a pleasant odor everywhere*

§ 20 Translation of aspect in Latin verbs [p. 75]

English has different distinctions of aspect from Latin, and, in order properly to express the meaning of the Latin, sometimes an English translation has to add expressions that are not formally in the Latin original. Thus

   a. The imperfective aspect of Latin may be translated into English as

      1. continuous action

> #1 **laudābās,** *you kept praising*
> #2 **laudās,** *you keep praising*
> #3 **laudābis,** *you will keep praising*

      2. incipient action

> **laudābās,** *you began to praise*

      3. repeated action

> **laudābās,** *you praised again and again*

      4. habitual action

> **laudābās,** *you used to praise*

      5. attempted action

> **laudābās,** *you tried to praise*

      6. progressive action

> **laudābās,** *you were praising*

Translation of aspect in verbs

b. The perfective aspect of Latin may often be translated into English as follows:

#4 **laudāverās**, *you had praised [in the past, but then stopped]*
#5 **laudāvistī**, *you have praised [by the present time and are now finished]*
#6 **laudāveris**, *you will have finished praising [in the future]* [1]

c. In narrative the #5 form **(laudāvistī)** is regularly used to describe an action in past time without implying that the events have been completed. Used in this way, **laudāvistī** may mean either *you have praised [and are now finished]* or simply *you praised*. In narrative the #2 tense is also sometimes used in the same way.

---

[1] The #6 tense is most often used in the "if" clause of a condition to express the idea that the action of the "if" clause must be completed before the action of the conclusion. Its English equivalent, however, is usually translated like a simple present, as in
   Malō afficiētur, si quis quārtam tetigerit. *If anyone touches [will have touched] the fourth part, he will be harmed by something evil.* II, 12, R50.

Basic text and clozes

Introduction

Because you have now progressed to a higher level, your work in Level Two contains proportionately more connected readings (like full poems, stories, and prose selections) and fewer individual *sententiae* than in Level One. The total amount that you read in Level Two, however, is appreciably greater than in Level One. For this reason, it would be unreasonable to expect you to remember the Basic Text in quite as much detail as you did before. The Unit Tests for Level Two reflect this in providing heavier cluing on the Basic Text questions and in limiting the number of Units you need to review each time.

However, the *Basic Sentences and Readings* are still the core of your Latin program, and studying them thoroughly is one of the most efficient ways for you to continue your progress in Latin. The Basic Sentences provide in a short space numerous illustrations of the new structures of each Unit: the Readings give you a chance both to practice these structures and to learn new vocabulary in an integrated context.

The Clozes in this section are designed to help you study the Basic Text in a directed and carefully organized fashion. They consist of the Basic Text for each Unit with certain key letters removed from each line. In the first set of clozes, two items are removed from each line; in the second and third sets, three items are removed.

Usually the items removed in the first set of clozes include the structure or structures that have just been taught in the Unit. For example, Unit One introduces deponent verbs. If you look at the first set of removals for Unit One, you will see that the deponent ending and the characteristic vowel of the verb have been removed. In the later sets, different items are taken out.

To see how this works out in more detail, look at the clozes for Reading 1. In the *first removal* for line 1, the dashes call attention to the fact that **sōlum** modifies **Sē** and the fact that **mirātur** is a deponent verb. In the *second removal* for this line (p. 152), **mirātur** is emphasized again through contrast with **amat** and **adōrat**; you must recall the different endings of regular and deponent verbs. In the *third removal* (p. 173), both **amat** and **sē** are removed, so that you must remember both the verb and its object. In this way, the clozes provide you with a more specific task and a more structured review than just "studying the text" might entail.

The recommended procedure for learning the Basic Text is as follows:
1. Complete a Unit in the programmed text.
2. Study the Basic Text of that Unit in the section before the clozes, referring back to the programmed text for any part whose meaning is unclear.
3. Work through the three sets of clozes, or "removals" in succession for the Unit you are studying until you feel you have mastered the material. If necessary, review the Basic Text again without the clozes.

These practice clozes are more difficult than the corresponding sections on the Unit Tests.
So if you do well in these sections, you should be able to do at least as well in the test questions on the Basic Text.

One reminder: *do not fill in the missing letters.* These clozes are an oral or mental review, not a written test. If you were to fill in the blanks, you could not review more than once. If you feel that you learn best only by writing, mark down the words or the entire lines on a separate piece of paper.

Basic sentences and readings

UNIT 1

S1   Lēgem nocēns verētur, Fortūnam innocēns. *Publilius Syrus* [Pg20]
S2   Stultus stulta loquitur. *Anonymous* — Stupid People say stupid things [a2]
S3   Crēscentem sequitur pecūniam cūra. *Horace*
S4   Nōn omnēs eadem mīrantur amantque. *Horace*
S5   Avārus, nisī cum moritur, nīl rēctē facit. *Publilius Syrus*
S6   Ē vīperā rursum vīpera nāscitur. *Anonymous*
S7   Sequitur superbia formam. *Anonymous*
S8   Cūrae levēs loquuntur, ingentēs stupent. *Seneca*
S9   Suum sequitur lūmen semper innocentia. *Publilius Syrus*
S10 Duōs quī sequitur leporēs neutrum capit. *Medieval*
S11   Quem dī dīligunt,
     adulēscēns moritur, dum valet, sentit, sapit.
                           Plautus

R1   Sē sōlum Labiēnus amat, mīrātur, adōrat:
      nōn modo sē sōlum, sē quoque sōlus amat.
            Joannes Audoenus (Renaissance)

UNIT 2

S12 Crēdō tē, Aeacidā, Rōmānōs vincere posse. *Ennius*
S13 Ēventus docuit fortēs Fortūnam juvāre. *Livy*

R2   Dīcis amōre tuī bellās ardēre puellās,
      quī faciem sub aquā, Sexte, natantis habēs.
                        Martial

R3 Dīcis formōsam, dīcis tē, Bassa, puellam.
    Istud, quae nōn est, dīcere, Bassa, solet.
                Martial

R4 Versiculōs in mē nārrātur scrībere Cinna.
    Nōn scrībit, cujus carmina nēmo legit.
                Martial

R5 Mentītur quī tē vitiōsum, Zōile, dīcit.
    Nōn vitiōsus homo es, Zōile, sed vitium.
                Martial

R6 Orbus es et locuplēs et Brūtō cōnsule nātus.
    Esse tibī vērās crēdis amīcitiās?
    Sunt vērae, sed quās juvenis, quās pauper habēbās.
    Quī novus est, mortem dīligit ille tuam.
                Martial

UNIT 3

S14 In prōverbium cessit sapientiam vīnō obumbrārī. *Pliny*
S15 Nēmō . . . regere potest nisī quī et regī. *Seneca*
S16 Et monēre et monērī proprium est vērae amīcitiae. *Cicero*
S17 Dulce et decōrum est prō patriā morī. *Horace*
S18 Et facere et patī fortia Rōmānum est. *Livy*
S19 Stultum est querī dē adversīs ubi culpa est tua. *Publilius Syrus*
S20 Ubī lībertās cecidit, audet līberē loquī nēmō. *Publilius Syrus*
S21 Ōre plēnō vel bibere vel loquī nec honestum est nec tūtum. *Petrus Alphonsus*

R7 Fūnera post septem nūpsit tibi Galla virōrum.
    Pīcentīne, Sequī vult, puto, Galla virōs.
                Martial

R8 Pauper vidērī Cinna vult. Et est pauper.
                Martial

UNIT 4

S22 Edāmus, bibāmus, gaudeāmus; post mortem nūlla voluptās. *Anonymous*
S23 Rapiāmus, amīcī, occāsiōnem dē diē. *Horace*
S24 Fīat jūstitia, ruat caelum. *Legal*
S25 Omnia vincit Amōr; et nōs cēdāmus Amōrī. *Vergil*

S26 Quī dēsīderat pācem praeparet bellum. *Vegetius*
S27 Ferās, nōn culpēs, quod mūtārī nōn potest. *Publilius Syrus*
S28 Amēs parentem, sī aequus est; sī aliter, ferās. *Publilius Syrus*
S29 Quī dedit beneficium taceat; nārret quī accēpit. *Seneca*
S30 Aut bibat aut abeat. *Cicero*

R9 Omnēs quās habuit, Fabiāne, Lycōris amīcās
    extulit. Uxōrī fīat amīca meae.
                        Martial

UNIT 5

S31 Nōn ut edam vīvō, sed ut vīvam edō. *Quintilian*

R10 Cūr nōn mitto meōs tibi, Pontiliāne, libellōs?
    Nē mihi tū mittās, Pontiliāne, tuōs.
                        Martial

R11 Exigis ut nostrōs dōnem tibi, Tucca, libellōs.
    Nōn faciam. Nam vīs vendere, nōn legere.
                        Martial

R12 Et jūdex petit et petit patrōnus.
Solvās cēnseo, Sexte, crēditōrī.
                        Martial

R13 Exigis ut dōnem nostrōs tibi, Quīnte, libellōs.
    Nōn habeō, sed habet bibliopōla Tryphōn.
"Aes dabō prō nūgīs et emam tua carmina sānus?
    Nōn" inquis "faciam tam fatuē." Nec egō.
                        Martial

R14 Semper agis causās et rēs agis, Attale, semper.
    Est, nōn est quod agās, Attale, semper agis.
Sī rēs et causae dēsunt, agis, Attale, mūlās.
    Attale, nē quod agās dēsit, agās animam.
                        Martial

R15 Sī meminī, fuerant tibi quattuor, Aelia, dentēs.
    Expulit ūna duōs tussis et ūna duōs.
Jam sēcūra potes tōtīs tussīre diēbus:
    nīl istīc quod agat tertia tussis habet.
                        Martial

UNIT 6

R16 Quid mihi reddat ager quaeris, Line, Nōmentānus?
  Hoc mihi reddit ager: tē, Line, nōn videō.
    Martial

R17 Nescio tam multīs quid scrībās, Fauste, puellīs.
  Hoc sciō, quod scrībit nūlla puella tibī.
    Martial

R18 Trīstis Athēnagorās nōn mīsit mūnera nōbīs
  quae mediō brūmae mittere mēnse solet.
  An sit Athēnagorās trīstis, Faustīne, vidēbō;
  mē certē trīstem fēcit Athēnagorās.
    Martial

R19 Scīs tē captārī; scīs hunc, quī captat, avārum;
  et scīs quī captat quid, Mariāne, velit.
  Tū tamen hunc tabulīs hērēdem, stulte, suprēmīs
  scrībis et esse tuō vīs, furiōse, locō.
  5 "Mūnera magna tamen mīsit." Sed mīsit in hāmō.
  Et piscātōrem piscis amāre potest?
  Hiccine dēflēbit vērō tua fāta dolōre?
  Sī cupis ut plōret, dēs, Mariāne, nihil.
    Martial

R20 Oculō Philaenis semper alterō plōrat.
  Quō fīat istud quaeritis modō? Lusca est.
    Martial

R21 Dēclāmās bellē, causās agis, Attice, bellē;
  historiās bellās, carmina bella facis;
  compōnis bellē mīmōs, epigrammata bellē;
  bellus grammaticus, bellus es astrologus;
  5 et bellē cantās et saltās, Attice, bellē;
  bellus es arte lyrae; bellus es arte pilae.
  Nīl bene cum faciās, faciās tamen omnia bellē.
  Vīs dīcam quid sīs? Magnus es ardaliō.
    Martial

UNIT 7

R22 Dē vulpe et ūvā

Famē coācta vulpēs altā in vīneā
ūvam appetēbat, summīs saliēns vīribus.
Quam tangere ut nōn potuit, discēdēns ait,
"Nōndum mātūra es; nōlo acerbam sūmere."

5 Quī, facere quae nōn possunt, verbīs ēlevant.
āscrībere hoc dēbēbunt exemplum sibī.
Phaedrus

R23 Dē vitiīs hominum

Pērās imposuit Juppiter nōbīs duās;
propriīs replētam vitiīs post tergum dedit;
aliēnīs ante pectus suspendit gravem.

Hāc rē vidēre nostra mala nōn possumus;
5 aliī simul dēlinquunt, cēnsōrēs sumus.
Phaedrus

R24 Vulpēs ad persōnam tragicam

Persōnam tragicam forte vulpēs vīderat.
"Ō quanta speciēs" inquit "cerebrum nōn habet!"

Hoc illīs dictum est quibus honōrem et glōriam
Fortūna tribuit, sēnsum commūnem abstulit.
Phaedrus

R25 Passer ad leporem cōnsiliātor

Sibi nōn cavēre et aliīs cōnsilium dare
stultum esse paucīs ostendāmus versibus.

Oppressum ab aquilā, flētūs et dantem gravēs,
leporem objūrgābat passer. "Ubī pernīcitās
5 nōta" inquit "illa est? Quid ita cessā'runt pedēs?"
Dum loquitur, ipsum accipiter necopīnum rapit
questūque vānō clāmitantem interficit.
Lepus sēmianimus: "Mortis ēn sōlācium!
Quī modo sēcūrus nostra irrīdēbās mala,
10 similī querēlā fāta dēplōrās tua."
Phaedrus

UNIT 8

R26 **Canis per fluvium carnem ferēns**

Āmittit meritō proprium quī aliēnum appetit.

Canis per flūmen carnem cum ferret natāns,
lymphārum in speculō vīdit simulācrum suum,
aliamque praedam ab alterō ferrī putāns,
5 ēripere voluit. Vērum dēcepta aviditās,
et quem tenēbat ōre dīmīsit cibum,
nec quem petēbat adeō potuit tangere.
Phaedrus

R27 **Mūli duo et latrōnēs**

Mūlī gravātī sarcinīs ībant duo;
ūnus ferēbat fiscōs cum pecūniā,
alter tumentēs multō saccōs hordeō.
Ille onere dīves celsā cervīce ēminet
5 clārumque collō jactat tintinnābulum;
comes quiētō sequitur et placidō gradū.
Subitō latrōnēs ex īnsidiīs advolant;
dīripiunt nummōs; neglegunt vīle hordeum;
interque caedem ferrō mūlum sauciant.
10 Spoliātus igitur cāsūs cum flēret suōs,
"Equidem" inquit alter "mē contemptum gaudeō;
nam nihil āmīsī nec sum laesus vulnere."

Hōc argūmentō tūta est hominum tenuitās;
magnae perīc'lō sunt opēs obnoxiae.
Phaedrus

UNIT 9

S32 Bona opīniō hominum tūtior pecūniā est. *Publilius Syrus*
S33 Vīlius argentum est aurō, virtūtibus aurum. *Horace*
S34 Tantō major fāmae sitis est quam virtūtis! *Juvenal*
S35 Intolerābilius nihil est quam fēmina dīves. *Juvenal*
S36 Quid clārius astrīs? *Motto*
S37 Sīmia quam similis turpissima bēstia nōbīs! *Ennius*
S38 Multō grātius venit quod facilī quam quod plēnā manū datur. *Seneca*

R28 **Rāna rupta et bōs**

  Inops, potentem dum vult imitārī, perit.

  In prātō quondam rāna cōnspexit bovem,
  et tācta invidiā tantae magnitūdinis
  rūgōsam īnflāvit pellem. Tum nātōs suōs
5 interrogāvit an bove esset lātior.
  Illī negā'runt. Rursus intendit cutem
  majōre nīsū, et similī quaesīvit modō
  quis major esset. Illī dīxērunt bovem.
  Novissimē indīgnāta, dum vult validius
10 īnflāre sēsē, ruptō jacuit corpore.
          Phaedrus

R29 Ad lapidem Torquātus habet praetōria quārtum;
      ad quārtum breve rūs ēmit Otācilius.
    Torquātus nitidās variō dē marmore thermās
      exstrūxit; cucumam fēcit Otācilius.
  5 Disposuit daphōna suō Torquātus in agrō;
      castaneās centum sēvit Otācilius.
    Cōnsule Torquātō, vīcī fuit ille magister;
      nōn minor in tantō vīsus honōre sibī.
    Grandis ut exiguam bōs rānam rūperat ōlim,
  10   sīc, puto, Torquātus rumpet Otācilium.
          Martial

R30 Omnēs aut vetulās habēs amīcās
    aut turpēs vetulīsque foediōrēs.
    Hās dūcis comitēs trahisque tēcum
    per convīvia, porticūs, theātra.
  5 Sīc formōsa, Fabulla, sīc puella es.
          Martial

R31 Petit Gemellus nūptiās Marōnillae
    et cupit et īnstat et precātur et dōnat.
    Adeōne pulchra est? Immō, foedius nīl est.
    Quid ergō in illā petitur et placet? Tussit.
          Martial

R32 Septima jam, Philerōs, tibi conditur uxor in agrō.
    Plūs nūllī, Philerōs, quam tibi reddit ager.
          Martial

R33 Sunt bona, sunt quaedam mediocria, sunt mala plūra
 quae legis hīc. Aliter nōn fit, Avīte, liber.
Martial

R34 Casta suō gladium cum trāderet Arria Paetō
 quem dē vīsceribus strīnxerat ipsa suīs,
 (sī qua fidēs) "Vulnus quod fēcī nōn dolet," inquit
 "sed tū quod faciēs, hoc mihi, Paete, dolet."
Martial

UNIT 10

S39 Frangar, nōn flectar. *Motto*
S40 Trahimur omnēs studiō laudis. *Cicero*
S41 Videō meliōra probōque, dēteriōra sequor. *Ovid*
S42 Prōgredimur quō dūcit quemque voluntās. *Lucretius*
S43 Nāscentēs morimur, fīnisque ab orīgine pendet. *Manilius*
S44 Tempora mūtantur, nōs et mūtāmur in illīs. *Borbonius (?)*

R35 Rumpitur invidiā quīdam, cārissime Jūlī,
 quod mē Rōma legit; rumpitur invidiā.
 Rumpitur invidiā quod turbā semper in omnī
 mōnstrāmur digitō; rumpitur invidiā.
5 Rumpitur invidiā tribuit quod Caesar uterque
 jūs mihi nātōrum; rumpitur invidiā.
 Rumpitur invidiā quod rūs mihi dulce sub urbe est
 parvaque in urbe domus; rumpitur invidiā.
 Rumpitur invidiā quod sum jūcundus amīcīs,
10 quod convīva frequēns; rumpitur invidiā.
 Rumpitur invidiā quod amāmur quodque probāmur.
 Rumpātur quisquis rumpitur invidiā.
Martial

R36   Quod fronte Selium nūbilā vidēs, Rūfe,
        quod ambulātor porticum terit sēram,
        lūgubre quiddam quod tacet piger vultus,
        quod paene terram nāsus indecēns tangit,
    5 quod dextrā pectus pulsat et comam vellit —
        nōn ille amīcī fāta lūget aut frātris;
        uterque nātus vīvit et precor vīvat;
        salva est et uxor sarcinaeque servīque;
        nihil colōnus vīlicusque dēcoxit.
    10 Maerōris igitur causa quae? Domī cēnat.
                                                    Martial

R37   Mīrāris veterēs, Vacerra, sōlōs
        nec laudās nisi mortuōs poētās.
        Īgnōscās petimus, Vacerra: tantī
        nōn est, ut placeam tibī, perīre.
                                                    Martial

R38   Nōn dōnem tibi cūr meōs libellōs
        ōrantī totiēns et exigentī
        mīrāris, Theodōre? Magna causa est:
        dōnēs tū mihi nē tuōs libellōs.
                                                    Martial

R39   Scrībere mē quereris, Vēlōx, epigrammata longa.
        Ipse nihil scrībis: tū breviōra facis.
                                                    Martial

R40   Nūbere vīs Prīscō. Nōn mīror, Paula; sapī'stī.
        Dūcere tē nōn vult Prīscus, et ille sapit.
                                                    Martial

R41   Uxōrem nōn vīs Pollam, nec Polla marītum
        tē vult. Bunne, sapis, nec minus illa sapit.
                                                John Parkhurst,
                                        Bishop of Norwich (1512-1575)

R42   Quod convīvāris sine mē tam saepe, Luperce,
        invēnī noceam quā ratiōne tibī.
        Īrāscor. Licet ūsque vocēs mittāsque rogēsque —
        "Quid faciēs?" inquis? Quid faciam? Veniam.
                                                    Martial

R43 Tū Sētīna quidem semper vel Massica pōnis,
       Pāpyle, sed rūmor tam bona vīna negat.
     Dīceris hāc factus caelebs quater esse lagōnā.
       Nec puto nec crēdō, Pāpyle, nec sitiō.
                                          Martial

UNIT 11

S45 Audī, vidē, tacē, sī vīs vīvere in pāce. *Medieval*
S46 Bene ferre magnam disce fortūnam. *Horace*
S47 Sī quid agis, prūdenter agās et respice fīnem. *Translation of Aesop*
S48 Dīvide et imperā. *Anonymous*

R44 Aegrōtās ūnō deciēns aut saepius annō;
       nec tibi sed nōbīs hoc, Polycharme, nocet.
     Nam quotiēns surgis, sōtēria poscis amīcōs.
       Sit pudor: aegrōtā jam, Polycharme, semel.
                                          Martial

R45 Nōn dē vī neque caede nec venēnō,
       sed līs est mihi dē tribus capellīs.
     Vīcīnī queror hās abesse fūrtō.
       Hoc jūdex sibi postulat probārī.
   5 Tū Cannās Mithridāticumque bellum
       et perjūria Pūnicī furōris
       et Sullās Mariōsque Mūciōsque
       magnā vōce sonās manūque tōtā.
     Jam dīc, Postume, dē tribus capellīs.
                                          Martial

R46 Cum mē captārēs, mittēbās mūnera nōbīs.
       Postquam cēpistī, dās mihi, Rūfe, nihil.
     Ut captum teneās, captō quoque mūnera mitte,
       dē caveā fugiat nē male pāstus aper.
                                          Martial

R47 **Lupus et agnus**

Ad rīvum eundem lupus et agnus vēnerant
siti compulsī. Superior stābat lupus,
longēque īnferior agnus. Tunc fauce improbā
latrō incitātus jūrgiī causam intulit.
5 "Cūr" inquit "turbulentam fēcistī mihī
aquam bibentī?" Lāniger contrā timēns:
"Quī possum, quaesō, facere quod quereris, lupe?
Ā tē dēcurrit ad meōs haustūs liquor."
Repulsus ille vēritātis vīribus,
10 "Ante hōs sex mēnsēs male" ait "dīxistī mihī."
Respondit agnus: "Equidem nātus nōn eram."
"Pater, Hercle, tuus," ille inquit "male dīxit mihī."
Atque ita correptum lacerat injūstā nece.

Haec propter illōs scrīpta est hominēs fābula
quī fictīs causīs innocentēs opprimunt.
Phaedrus

UNIT 12

S49 Ēn ego Fortūna! Sī stārem sorte sub ūnā
et nōn mūtārer, numquam "Fortūna" vocārer.
Medieval

S50 Sī quem barbātum faceret sua barba beātum,
in mundī circō nōn esset sānctior hircō.
Medieval

S51 Sī foret in terrīs, rīdēret Dēmocritus. *Horace*

R48 Nūbere Paula cupit nōbīs; ego dūcere Paulam
nōlō: anus est. Vellem, sī magis esset anus.
Martial

R49 **Vulpēs et corvus**

    Quī sē laudārī gaudet verbīs subdolīs,
    ferē dat poenās turpī paenitentiā.

    Cum dē fenestrā corvus raptum cāseum
    comēsse vellet, celsā residēns arbore,
5 vulpēs invīdit; deinde sīc coepit loquī:
    "Ō quī tuārum, corve, pennārum est nitor!
    Quantum decoris corpore et vultū geris!
    Sī vōcem habērēs, nūlla prior āles foret!"
    At ille stultus, dum vult vōcem ostendere,
10 lātō ōre ēmīsit cāseum, quem celeriter
    dolōsa vulpēs avidīs rapuit dentibus.
    Tum dēmum ingemuit corvī dēceptus stupor.
                                 Phaedrus

R50 **Vacca, capella, ovis, et leō**

    Numquam est fidēlis cum potente societās:
    testātur haec fābella prōpositum meum.

    Vacca et capella et patiēns ovis injūriae
    sociī fuēre cum leōne in saltibus.
5 Hī cum cēpissent cervum vastī corporis,
    sīc est locūtus, partibus factīs, leō:
    "Ego prīmam tollō, nōminor quoniam 'Leō.'
    Secundam, quia sum fortis, tribuētis mihī.
    Tum quia plūs valeō, mē sequētur tertia.
10 Malō afficiētur, sī quis quārtam tetigerit."
    Sīc tōtam praedam sōla improbitās abstulit.
                                 Phaedrus

R51 Vulpēs et caper

Homō in perīc'lum simul ac vēnit callidus,
reperīre effugium quaerit alterius malō.

Cum dēcidisset vulpēs in puteum īnscia
et altiōre clauderētur margine,
5 dēvēnit hircus sitiēns in eundem locum.
Simul rogāvit esset an dulcis liquor
et cōpiōsus, illa fraudem mōliēns:
"Dēscende, amīce! Tanta bonitās est aquae
voluptās ut satiārī nōn possit mea."
10 Immīsit sē barbātus. Tum vulpēcula
ēvāsit puteō, nīxa celsīs cornibus,
hircumque clausō līquit haerentem vadō.
Phaedrus

UNIT 13

S52 Moritūrī tē salūtāmus. *Based on Suetonius*

R52 Anus ad amphoram

Anus jacēre vīdit ēpōtam amphoram,
adhūc Falernā faece ē testā nōbilī
odōrem quae jūcundum lātē spargeret.
Hunc postquam tōtīs avida trāxit nāribus:
5 "Ō suāvis anima! Quāle in tē dīcam bonum
antehāc fuisse, tālēs cum sint reliquiae?"
Hoc quō pertineat dīcet quī mē nōverit.
Phaedrus

R53 Īnscrīpsit tumulīs septem scelerāta virōrum
sē fēcisse Chloē. Quid pote simplicius?
Martial

R54 Jactat inaequālem Matho mē fēcisse libellum.
Si vērum est, laudat carmina nostra Mathō.
Aequālēs scrībit librōs Calvīnus et Umber:
aequālis liber est, Crētice, quī malus est.
Martial

R55 Lupus et vulpēs, jūdice sīmiō

Quīcumque turpī fraude semel innōtuit,
etiam sī vērum dīcit, āmittit fidem.
Hocc attestātur brevis Aesōpī fābula.

Lupus arguēbat vulpem fūrtī crīmine;
5 negābat illa sē esse culpae proximam.
Tunc jūdex inter illōs sēdit sīmius.
Uterque causam cum perōrā'ssent suam,
dīxisse fertur sīmius sententiam:
"Tū nōn vidēris perdidisse quod petis;
10 tē crēdō surripuisse quod pulchrē negās.
Phaedrus

R56 Rānae ad sōlem

Vīcīnī fūris celebrēs vīdit nūptiās
Aesōpus et continuō nārrāre coepit:
"Uxōrem quondam Sōl cum vellet dūcere,
clāmōrem rānae sustulēre ad sīdera.
5 Convīciō permōtus quaerit Juppiter
causam querēlae. Quaedam tum stāgnī incola
'Nunc' inquit 'omnēs ūnus exūrit lacūs
cōgitque miserās āridā sēde ēmorī.
Quidnam futūrum est, sī creā'rit līberōs?' "
Phaedrus

UNIT 14

S53 Vigilāte et ōrāte. *Anonymous*
S54 Quaerite Dominum, et vīvet anima vestra. *Anonymous*
S55 Dum Fāta sinunt, vīvite laetī. *Seneca*

R57 **Aquila, fēlēs, et aper**

    Aquila in sublīmī quercū nīdum fēcerat;
    fēlēs cavernam nacta in mediā pepererat;
    sūs, nemoris cultrīx, fētum ad īmam posuerat.
    Tum fortuitum fēlēs contubernium
5 fraude et scelestā sīc ēvertit malitiā.
    Ad nīdum scandit volucris. "Perniciēs" ait
    "tibī parātur, forsan et miserae mihī!
    Nam, fodere terram quod vidēs cottīdiē
    aprum īnsidiōsum, quercum vult ēvertere,
10 ut nostram in plānō facile prōgeniem opprimat."
    Terrōre offūsō et perturbātīs sēnsibus,
    dērēpit ad cubīle saetōsae suis.
    "Magnō" inquit "in perīc'lō sunt nātī tuī.
    Nam, simul exieris pāstum cum tenerō grege,
15 aquila est parāta rapere porcellōs tibī."
    Hunc quoque timōre postquam complēvit locum,
    dolōsa tūtō condidit sēsē cavō.
    Inde ēvagāta noctū suspēnsō pede;
    ubi ēscā sē replēvit et prōlem suam,
20 pavōrem simulāns prōspicit tōtō diē.
    Ruīnam metuēns aquila rāmīs dēsidet;
    aper rapīnam vītāns nōn prōdit forās.
    Quid multa? Inediā sunt cōnsūmptī cum suīs
    fēlisque catulīs lārgam praebuērunt dapem.

25 Quantum homo bilinguis saepe concinnet malī
    documentum habēre hinc stulta crēdulitās potest.
                                                 Phaedrus

R58 **Canis fidēlis**

Repente līberālis stultīs grātus est;
vērum perītīs irritōs tendit dolōs.

Nocturnus cum fūr pānem mīsisset canī,
objectō temptāns an cibō posset capī,
5 "Heus!" inquit "linguam vīs meam praeclūdere,
nē lātrem prō rē dominī? Multum falleris.
Namque ista subita mē jubet benīgnitās
vigilāre, faciās nē meā culpā lucrum."
Phaedrus

R59 Nīl mihi dās vīvus; dīcis post fāta datūrum.
Sī nōn es stultus, scīs, Maro, quid cupiam.
Martial

R60 Ā fēminīs utcumque spoliārī virōs
(ament, amentur) nempe exemplīs discimus.

Aetātis mediae quendam mulier nōn rudis
tenēbat (annōs cēlāns ēlegantiā)
5 animōsque ejusdem pulchra juvenis cēperat.
Ambae, vidērī dum volunt illī parēs,
capillōs hominī legere coepēre in vicem.
Quī sē putāret fingī cūrā mulierum
calvus repente factus est. Nam funditus
10 cānōs puella, nigrōs anus ēvellerat.
Phaedrus

R61 Quod lānā caput alligās, Charīne,
nōn aurēs tibi sed dolent capillī.
Martial

UNIT 15

R62 **Soror et frāter**

Praeceptō monitus saepe tē cōnsīderā.

Habēbat quīdam fīliam turpissimam
īdemque īnsīgnem pulchrā faciē fīlium.
Hī speculum, in cathedrā mātris ut positum fuit,
5 puerīliter lūdentēs forte īnspexērunt.
Hic sē formōsum jactat; illa īrāscitur
nec glōriantis sustinet frātris jocōs,
accipiēns (Quid enim?) cūncta in contumēliam.
Ergō ad patrem dēcurrit laesūra in vicem
10 magnāque invidiā crīminātur fīlium,
vir nātus quod rem fēminārum tetigerit.
Amplexus ille utrumque et carpēns ōscula
dulcemque in ambōs cāritātem partiēns:
"Cottīdiē" inquit "speculō vōs ūtī volō:
15 tū formam nē corrumpās nēquitiae malīs;
tū faciem ut istam mōribus vincās bonīs."
Phaedrus

R63 **Cervus ad fontem**

Laudātīs ūtiliōra quae contempserīs
saepe invenīrī testis haec nārrātiō est.

Ad fontem cervus, cum bibisset, restitit
et in liquōre vīdit effigiem suam.
5 Ibi dum rāmōsa mīrāns laudat cornua
crūrumque nimiam tenuitātem vituperat,
vēnantum subitō vōcibus conterritus
per campum fugere coepit et cursū levī
canēs ēlūsit. Silva tum excēpit ferum,
10 in quā retentīs impedītus cornibus
lacerārī coepit morsibus saevīs canum.
Tunc moriēns ēdidisse vōcem hanc dīcitur:
"Ō mē īnfēlīcem! Quī nunc dēmum intellegō
ūtilia mihī quam fuerint quae dēspexeram
15 et quae laudā'ram, quantum lūctūs habuerint."
Phaedrus

R64   Leō senex, aper, taurus, et asinus

Quīcumque āmīsit dignitātem prīstinam,
ignāvīs etiam jocus est in cāsū gravī.

Dēfectus annīs et dēsertus vīribus
leō cum jacēret spīritum extrēmum trahēns,
5 aper fulmineīs spūmāns vēnit dentibus
et vindicāvit ictū veterem injūriam.
Īnfēstīs taurus mox cōnfōdit cornibus
hostīle corpus. Asinus, ut vīdit ferum
impūne laedī, calcibus frontem extūdit.
10 At ille exspīrāns: "Fortīs indignē tulī
mihi īnsultāre; tē, nātūrae dēdecus,
quod ferre cōgor, certē bis videor morī."
Phaedrus

R65   Equus et aper

Equus sēdāre solitus quō fuerat sitim,
dum sēsē aper volūtat turbāvit vadum.
Hinc orta līs est. Sonipēs īrātus ferō
auxilium peti'it hominis. Quem dorsō levāns
5 rediit ad hostem laetus. Hunc tēlīs eques
postquam interfēcit, sīc locūtus trāditur:
"Laetor tulisse auxilium mē precibus tuīs.
Nam praedam cēpī et didicī quam sīs ūtilis."
Atque ita coēgit frēnōs invītum patī.
10 Tum maestus ille: "Parvae vindictam reī
dum quaerō dēmēns, servitūtem repperī."

Haec īrācundōs admonēbit fābula
impūne potius laedī quam dēdī alterī.
Phaedrus

UNIT 16

S56   Sī tacuissēs, philosophus mānsissēs. *Attributed to Boethius*
S57   Hectora quis nō'sset, sī fēlīx Troja fuisset? *Ovid*
S58   Ō fīlī cāre, nōlī nimis altē volāre. *Medieval*
S59   Nōlī mē tangere. *John*
S60   Nōlī barbam vellere mortuō leōnī. *Martial*
S61   Contrā verbōsōs nōlī contendere verbīs. *Dionysius Cato*

R66 Asinus et leō vēnantēs

Virtūtis expers, verbīs jactāns glōriam.
īgnōtōs fallit, nōtīs est dērīsuī.

Vēnārī, asellō comite, cum vellet leō,
contēxit illum frutice et admonuit simul
5 ut īnsuētā vōce terrēret ferās,
fugientēs ipse exciperet. Hīc aurītulus
clāmōrem subitō tollit tōtīs vīribus
novōque turbat bēstiās mīrāculō.
Quae, dum paventēs exitūs nōtōs petunt,
10 leōnis afflīguntur horrendō impetū.
Quī, postquam caede fessus est, asinum ēvocat
jubetque vōcem premere. Tunc ille īnsolēns:
"Quālis vidētur opera tibī vōcis meae?"
"Īnsīgnis" inquit "sīc ut, nisi nō' ssem tuum
15 animum genusque, similī fūgissem metū."

Phaedrus

R67

Quid Deus intendat, nōlī perquīrere sorte;
quid statuat dē tē, sine tē dēlīberat ille.

Dionysius Cato

R68 Mustēla et homō

Mustēla ab homine prēnsa, cum īnstantem necem
effugere vellet, "Parce, quaeso," inquit "mihī,
quae tibi molestīs mūribus pūrgō domum."
Respondit ille, "Facerēs sī causā meā,
5 grātum esset et dedissem veniam supplicī.
Nunc, quia labōrās ut fruāris reliquiīs
quās sunt rōsūrī, simul et ipsōs dēvorēs,
nōlī imputāre vānum beneficium mihī."
Atque ita locūtus improbam lētō dedit.

10 Hoc in sē dictum dēbent illī āgnōscere,
quōrum prīvāta servit ūtilitās sibī,
et meritum ināne jactant imprūdentibus.

Phaedrus

R69 Quisquis Flāminiam teris, viātor,
　　　nōlī nōbile praeterīre marmor.
　　　Urbis dēliciae salēsque Nīlī,
　　　ars et grātia, lūsus et voluptās,
　5　Rōmānī decus et dolar theātrī
　　　atque omnēs Venerēs Cupīdinēsque
　　　hōc sunt condita quō Paris sepulchrō.
　　　　　　　　　　　　　　Martial

R70 Cum tua nōn ēdās, carpis mea carmina, Laelī.
　　　Carpere vel nōlī nostra vel ēde tua.
　　　　　　　　　　　　　　Martial

R71 Ūndeciēns ūnā surrēx'tī, Zōile, cēnā,
　　　　et mūtāta tibi est synthesis ūndeciēns,
　　　sūdor inhaerēret madidā nē veste retentus
　　　　et laxam tenuis laederet aura cutem.
　5　Quā rē ego nōn sūdō, quī tēcum, Zōile, cēnō?
　　　Frīgus enim magnum synthesis ūna facit.
　　　　　　　　　　　　　　Martial

UNIT 17

S62　Carthāgō dēlenda est. *Cato (adapted)*
S63　Pānis fīliōrum nōn objiciendus canibus. *Matthew*
S64　Dēlīberandum est saepe, statuendum est semel. *Publilius Syrus*
S65　Diū apparandum est bellum, ut vincās celerius. *Publilius Syrus*
S66　Vitium uxōris aut tollendum aut ferendum est. *Varro*

UNIT 18

S67　Dēlīberandō discitur sapientia. *Publilius Syrus*
S68　Dēlīberandō saepe perit occāsiō. *Publilius Syrus*
S69　Negandī causa avārō numquam dēficit. *Publilius Syrus*
S70　Legendī semper occāsiō est, audiendī nōn semper. *Pliny the Younger*
S71　Breve . . . tempus aetātis; satis est longum ad bene honestēque vīvendum. *Cicero*
S72　Jūstitia est cōnstāns et perpetua voluntās jūs suum cuique tribuendī. *Justinian*
S73　Male imperandō summum imperium āmittitur. *Publilius Syrus*

Unit 21

R72 Nihil . . . sine ratiōne faciendum est. *Seneca*
R73 Citō scrībendō nōn fit ut bene scrībātur; bene scrībendō fit ut citō. *Quintilian*
R74 Sapientia . . . ars vīvendī putanda est. *Cicero*
R75 Ratiōne, nōn vī, vincenda adulēscentia est. *Publilius Syrus*
R76 Nihil agendō hominēs male agere discunt. *Marcus Porcius Cato*

UNIT 19

S74 Nēmō est tam fortis quīn reī novitāte perturbētur. *Caesar*
S75 Nōn licet in bellō bis peccāre. *Anonymous*
S76 Semel in annō licet īnsānīre. *Anonymous*
S77 Quod licet Jovī nōn licet bovī. *Anonymous*
S78 Ēsse oportet ut vīvās, nōn vīvere ut edās. *Anonymous*

UNIT 21

S79 Spectātum veniunt; veniunt spectentur ut ipsae. *Ovid*

Readings in Caesar

Dē Bellō Gallicō, Book One

		Unit	Frame
Chapter 1:	Gallia est omnis dīvīsa . . .	17	72
Chapter 2:	Apud Helvētiōs longē nōbilissimus . . .	18	166
Chapter 3:	Hīs rēbus adductī . . .	19	37, 46
Chapter 4:	Ea rēs est Helvētiīs . . .	19	116
Chapter 5:	Post ejus mortem nihilō minus . . .	20	19
Chapter 6:	Erant omīnō itinera duo . . .	20	45
Chapter 7:	Caesarī cum id nūntiātum esset . . .	20	76
Chapter 8:	Intereā eā legiōne . . .	21	11
Chapter 9:	Relinquēbātur ūna per Sēquanōs via . . .	21	26
Chapter 10:	Caesarī renūntiātur . . .	21	54
Chapter 11:	Helvētiī jam per angustiās . . .	21	119
Chapter 12:	Flūmen est Arar . . .	21	165
Chapter 13:	Hōc proeliō factō . . .	22	102
Chapter 14:	Hīs Caesar ita respondit . . .	22	161
Chapter 15:	Posterō diē castra ex eō locō . . .	23	20
Chapter 16:	Interim cottīdiē Caesar . . .	23	46
Chapter 17:	Tum dēmum Liscus . . .	23	66
Chapter 18:	Caesar hāc ōrātiōne Liscī . . .	23	80
Chapter 19:	Quibus rēbus cognitīs . . .	23	107

Chapter 20:	Dīviciācus multīs cum lacrimīs . . .	23	131
Chapter 21:	Eōdem diē ab explōrātōribus . . .	23	157
Chapter 22:	Prīmā lūce, cum summus mōns . . .	23	175
Chapter 23:	Postrīdiē ejus diēī . . .	24	6
Chapter 24:	Postquam id animum advertit . . .	24	41
Chapter 25:	Caesar, prīmum suō, deinde omnium . . .	24	67
Chapter 26:	Ita ancipitī proeliō diū . . .	24	118
Chapter 27:	Helvētiī omnium rērum inopiā . . .	24	134
Chapter 28:	Quod ubī Caesar resciit . . .	24	142
Chapter 29:	In castrīs Helvētiōrum tabulae . . .	24	162

Clozes
first removal

UNIT 1

S1 Lēg__ nocēns ver_____, Fortūnam innocēns. *Publilius Syrus*
S2 Stult__ stulta loqu_____. *Anonymous*
S3 Crēscentem sequ_____ pecūn_____ cūra. *Horace*
S4 Nōn omnēs eadem mīr_____ am__que. *Horace*
S5 Avār__, nisī cum mor_____, nīl rēctē facit. *Publilius Syrus*
S6 Ē vīpe__ rursum vīpera nāsc_____. *Anonymous*
S7 Sequ_____ superbia form__. *Anonymous*
S8 Cūrae levēs loqu_____, ingentēs stup_____. *Seneca*
S9 Su__ sequ_____ lūmen semper innocentia. *Publilius Syrus*
S10 Duōs quī sequ_____ leporēs neutr__ capit. *Medieval*

S11   Quem dī dīlig_____,
      adulēscēns mor_____, dum valet, sentit, sapit.
                                  Platus

R1 Sē sōl__ Labiēnus amat, mīr_____, adōrat:
      nōn modo sē sōl__, sē quoque sōl__ amat.
                    Joannes Audoenus (Renaissance)

UNIT 2

S12 Crēdō ___, Aeacidā, Rōmānōs vincere pos__. *Ennius*
S13 Ēventus docuit fortēs Fortūn__ juv_____. *Livy*

R2 Dīcis amōre tuī bellās ard_____ puell__,
      quī faciem sub aquā, Sexte, natant__ hab__.
                                  Martial

R3 Dīcis formōsam, d_____ tē, Bassa, puell___.
    Ist___, quae nōn est, dīcere, Bassa, sol___.
                                                    Martial

R4 Versiculōs in mē nārrā_____ scrīb_____ Cinna.
    Nōn scrībit, cu_____ carm_____ nēmo legit.
                                                    Martial

R5 Ment_____ quī tē vitiōs___, Zōile, dīcit.
    Nōn viti_____ homo es, Zōile, sed viti___.
                                                    Martial

R6 Orb___ es et locupl___ et Brūtō cōnsule nātus.
    Es___ tibī vērās crēdis amīciti___?
    Sunt vērae, sed qu___ juvenis, quās pauper habē___s.
    Quī nov___ est, mort___ dīligit ille tuam.
                                                    Martial

UNIT 3

S14 In prōverbium cessit sapienti___ vīnō obumbrā___. *Pliny*
S15 Nēmō . . . regere pot_____ nisī quī et r_____. *Seneca*
S16 Et monēre et mon_____ proprium est vērae amīciti___. *Cicero*
S17 Dulce et decōr___ est prō patriā mor___. *Horace*
S18 Et fac_____ et pat___ fortia Rōmānum est. *Livy*
S19 Stult___ est quer___ dē adversīs ubi culpa est tua. *Publilius Syrus*
S20 Ubī lībertās cecidit, a___et līberē loqu___ nēmō. *Publilius Syrus*
S21 Ōre plēnō vel bib_____ vel loqu___ nec honestum est nec tūtum. *Petrus Alphonsus*

R7 Fūn_____ post septem nūpsit t_____ Galla virōrum,
    Pīcentīne. Sequ___ vult, puto, Galla vir___.
                                                    Martial

R8 Pauper vidē___ Cinna vult. Et est p_____.
                                                    Martial

UNIT 4

S22 Edāmus, bib_____, gaudē_____; post mortem nūlla voluptās. *Anonymous*
S23 Rapi___mus, amīcī, occāsion_____ dē diē. *Horace*
S24 Fī___ jūstitia, ru___ caelum. *Legal*
S25 Omn___ vincit Amōr; et nōs cēd_____ Amōrī. *Vergil*

First removal: unit 5

S26　Quī dēsīder_t pācem praepar_t bellum. *Vegetius*
S27　Fer_s, nōn culp_s, quod mūtārī nōn potest. *Publilius Syrus*
S28　Am_s parentem, sī aequus est; sī aliter, fer_s. *Publilius Syrus*
S29　Quī dedit beneficium tac__t; nārr_t quī accēpit. *Seneca*
S30　Aut bib_t aut ab__t. *Cicero*

R9　Omnēs qu__ habu__, Fabiāne, Lycōris amīcās
　　　extulit. Uxōrī f__t amīca me__.
　　　　　　　　　　　　　　　　　Martial

UNIT 5

S31　Nōn __ edam vīvō, sed ut vīv_ edō. *Quintilian*

R10　Cūr nōn mittō me__ tibi, Pontiliāne, libell__?
　　　Nē mihi tū mitt_s, Pontiliāne, tu__.
　　　　　　　　　　　　　　　　　Martial

R11　Exigis __ nostrōs dōn__ tibi, Tucca, libellōs.
　　　Nōn faci__. Nam vīs vendere, nōn leg__.
　　　　　　　　　　　　　　　　　Martial

R12　Et j__x petit et p____ patrōnus.
　　　Solv_ cēnseō, Sexte, crēditōr_.
　　　　　　　　　　　　　　　　　Martial

R13　Exigis ut dōn__ nostr__ tibi, Quīnte, libellōs.
　　　Nōn habeō, sed habe_ bibliopōl_ Tryphōn.
　　　"Aes dabō prō nūg__ et emam tua carm____ sānus?
　　　Nōn" inqu__ "faciam tam fatu_." Nec egō.
　　　　　　　　　　　　　　　　　Martial

R14　Semper ag__ causās et rēs ag__, Attale, semper.
　　　Est, nōn est quod ag__, Attale, semper ag__.
　　　Sī rēs et causae dēsunt, ag__, At____, mūlās.
　　　Attale, nē quod ag__ dēsit, ag__ animam.
　　　　　　　　　　　　　　　　　Martial

R15　Sī meminī, fuerant t__ quattuor, Aelia, dent__.
　　　Expulit ūna duōs tussis et ūn_ du_.
　　　Jam sēcūra pot__ tōtīs tuss__ diēbus:
　　　　nīl ist_c quod ag_t tertia tussis habet.
　　　　　　　　　　　　　　　　　Martial

UNIT 6

R16   Qu___ mihi redd__t ager quaeris, Line, Nōmentānus?
     H___ mihi redd__t ager: tē, Line, nōn videō.
                                             Martial

R17   Nescio tam multīs qu___ scrīb___, Fauste, puellīs.
     Hoc sciō, qu___ scrīb___ nūlla puella tibī.
                                             Martial

R18   Trīst___ Athēnagorās nōn mīsit mūnera nō_____
     quae medi__ brūmae mittere mēnse sol___.
     An s___ Athēnagorās trīstis Faustīne, vidē___;
     mē certē trīst___ fēc___ Athēnagorās.
                                             Martial

R19   Scīs tē capt_____; scīs hunc, quī captat, avār___;
     et scīs quī c_____ quid, Mariāne, vel___.
     Tū tamen hunc tabul___ hērēdem, stulte, suprēm___
     scrībis et e___e tuō v___, furiōse, locō.
   5 "Mūnera magna tamen mīsit." Sed m_____t in hām__.
     Et piscā_____ piscis am___ potest?
     Hiccine dēflēb___ vērō tua fāta dolōr___?
     Sī cupis ut plōr__t, d__s, Mariāne, nihil.
                                             Martial

R20   Oc____ Philaenis semper alt____ plōrat.
     Quō fī___ istu__ quaeritis mo___? Lusca est.
                                             Martial

R21   Dēclāmās bell__, causās agis, Attice, bell__;
     historiās bell___, carmina bell__ facis;
     compōnis bell__ mīmōs, epigrammata bell__;
     bell___ grammaticus, bell___ es astrologus;
   5 et bell__ cantās et saltās, Attice, bell__;
     bell___ es arte lyrae; bell___ es arte pilae.
     Nīl ben__ cum faciās, faciās tamen omnia bell__.
     Vīs dīcam quid s___? Magn____ es ardaliō.
                                             Martial

First removal: unit 6

R22 **Dē vulp_ et ūv_**

    Fam__ coācta vulpēs altā in vīn___
    ūvam appetēbat, summ__ saliēns vīr_____.
    Qu__ tang_____ ut nōn potuit, discēdēns ait,
    "Nōndum mātūra es; nōlo acerb__ sūm____."

  5 Quī, fac_____ quae nōn possunt, verb__ ēlevant,
    āscrīb_____ hoc dēbēbunt exemplum s____.
                                  Phaedrus

R23 **Dē viti__ homin__**

    Pēr__ imposuit Juppiter nōbīs du__:
    propri__ replētam viti__ post tergum dedit;
    aliēn__ ante pect__ suspendit gravem.

    Hāc rē vid_____ nostra mala nōn p__sumus;
  5 aliī s____l dēlinquunt, cēnsōr__ sumus.
                                  Phaedrus

R24 **Vulp__ ad persōnam trag_____**

    Pers_____ tragicam forte v_____ vīderat.
    "Ō quanta speciēs" inqu__ "cerebr__ nōn habet!"

    Hoc ill__ dictum est quibus honōr__ et glōriam
    Fortūna tribuit, sēn__ commūnem abs____it.
                                  Phaedrus

R25 **Passer ad lepor__ cōnsiliā__**

    S____ nōn cavēre et aliīs cōn_____ dare
    stultum esse paucīs ostend____s versi____.

    Oppressum ab aqu_____, flēt__ et dantem gravēs,
    l_____m objūragābat passer. "Ubī pernīci____
  5 nōta" in_____ "illa est? Quid ita cessā'runt p__ēs?"
    Dum loquitur, ips__ accipiter necopīn__ rapit
    questūque vānō clām____ntem in__ficit.
    Lepus sēmi____mus: "Mort__ ēn sōlācium!
    Quī modo sēcūr__ nostra irrīdēb__ mala,
  10 simil__ querēlā fāta dēplōr__ tua."
                                  Phaedrus

UNIT 8

R26 **Canis per fluvium carn___ fer__s**

Āmittit merit_ propri___ quī aliēnum appetit.

Canis per flūm___ carnem cum fer__t natāns,
lymphā___ in speculō vīdit simulācrum su___,
ali__que praedam ab alterō fer___ putāns,
5 ēripe___ voluit. Vērum dēcepta avidi___,
et qu___ tenēbat ōre dīmīsit cibu__,
nec qu___ petēbat adeō potu___ tangere.
        Phaedrus

R27 **Mūl_ duo ___ latrōn___**

Mū___ gravātī sarcin___ ībant duo;
ūnus ferēbat fīsc___ cum pec_____,
alter tument___ multō sacc___ hordeō.
Ille onere dīves cels_ cervīce ēminet
5 clār__que collō jactat tintinnābu_____;
comes quiē___ sequitur et placidō gra___.
Subit_ latrōnēs ex īnsidi___ advolant;
dīripiunt numm___; neglegunt vīl_ hordeum;
interque caed___ ferrō mūlu_ sauciant.
10 Spoliātus igitur cās___ cum flē__t suōs,
"Equidem" inqu___ alter "mē contemp_____ gaudeō;
na_ ni___ āmīsī nec sum laesus vulnere."

Hōc argūme_____ tūta est hominum tenui___;
magn___ perīc'l_ sunt opēs obnoxiae.
        Phaedrus

UNIT 9

S32 Bona opīniō hominum tūt___ pecūni_ est. *Publilius Syrus*
S33 Vīl___ argentum est aurō, virtūtī ___ aurum. *Horace*
S34 Tantō maj___ fāmae sitis est qu___ virtūtis! *Juvenal*
S35 Intolerābil___ nihil est qu__ fēmina dīves. *Juvenal*
S36 Quid clār___ astr___? *Motto*
S37 Sīmia quam similis turpi____ma bēstia n___is! *Ennius*
S38 Mult_ grāt___ venit quod facilī quam quod plēnā manū datur. *Seneca*

First removal: unit 9

R28 **Rā—— rupta et bō——**

   Inops, potent—— dum vult imitā——, perit.

   In prātō quondam rāna cōnsp——it bov——,
   et tācta invid—— tantae magnitūdin——
   rūgōs—— īnflāvit pell——. Tum nātōs suōs
5 interrogāvit a—— bov—— esset lātior.
   Illī negā'——. Rursus intendit cut——
   majōre nīs——, et similī quaesīvit mo——
   quis maj—— esset. Illī dīxērunt bov——.
   Novissim—— indīgnāta, dum vult valid——
10 īnflā—— sēsē, rup—— jacuit corpore.
                                    Phaedrus

R29 Ad lapid—— Torquātus habet praetōri—— quārtum;
       ad quārt——, brev—— rūs ēmit Otācilius.
    Torquātus nitid—— variō dē marmore therm——
       exstrūx——; cucumam fēc—— Otācilius.
5   Disposuit dāphnōn—— suō Torquātus in ag——;
       castane—— centum sēvit O————lius.
    Cōns—— Torquātō, vīc—— fuit ille magister;
       nōn min—— in tantō vīsus honō—— sibī.
    Grand——s ut exigu—— bōs rānam rūperat ōlim,
       sīc, puto, Torquātus rump——t Otācil——.
                                    Martial

R30 Omn—— aut vetulās habēs amīc——
       aut turpēs vetul——que foedi——es.
    Hās du——s comitēs trahisque tēc——
       per convīv——, portic——, theātra.
5   Sīc form——a, Fabulla, sīc pu————a es.
                                    Martial

R31 Petit Gemellus nūpti—— Marōnill——
       et cupit et īnst—— et prec—————— et dōnat.
    Ad——ne pulchra est? Immō, foed—— nīl est.
    Quid ergō in illā peti—— et placet? Tus——.
                                    Martial

R32 Septi—— jam, Philerōs, t—— conditur uxor in agrō.
       Pl—— nūl——, Philerōs, quam tibi reddit ager.
                                    Martial

R33 Sunt bona, sunt quaedam medi___ria, sunt mala plū___
    quae legis h___. Alit___ nōn fit, Avīte, liber.
                                                    Martial

R34 Casta su___ gladium cum trād___t Arria Paetō
    quem dē vīscer_____ strīnxerat ipsa su___,
    (sī qua fidēs) "Vulnus qu___ fē___ nōn dolet," inquit
    "sed tū quod faci___, hoc mi___, Paete, dolet."
                                                    Martial

UNIT 10

S39 Frang___, nōn flect___. *Motto*
S40 Trahi___ omnēs studiō laud___. *Cicero*
S41 Videō meliōra probōque, dēter___a sequ___. *Ovid*
S42 Prōgred_____ quō dūcit qu___que voluntās. *Lucretius*
S43 Nāscentēs mori_____, fīnisque ab orīgine pe___t. *Manilius*
S44 Tempora mūta_____, nōs et mūtā___ in illīs. *Borbonius (?)*

R35 Rump_____ invid___ quīdam, cārissime Jūlī,
    quod m___ Rō___ legit; rumpitur invidiā.
    Rumpitur invidiā quod turb___ semper in omn___
    mōnstrā_____ digitō; rumpitur inv_____.
 5 Rumpitur invidiā tribuit qu___ Caesar ut___que
    j___ mihi nātō___; rumpitur invidiā.
    Rumpitur invidiā qu___ rūs mihi dul___ sub urbe est
    parv___que in urbe dom___; rumpitur invidiā.
    Rumpitur invidiā qu___ sum jūcundus amīc___.
 10   qu___ convīva frequē___; rumpitur invidiā.
    Rumpitur invidiā qu___ amā_____ quodque probāmur.
    Rump___tur quisqu___ rumpitur invidiā.
                                                    Martial

R36 Qu___ fro___e Selium nūbilā vidēs, Rūfe,
    qu___ ambulātor porticum terit sēr___,
    lūgubre quid___m qu___ tacet piger vultus,
    qu___ p___ne terram nāsus indecēns tangit,
 5 qu___ dextrā pect___ pulsat et comam vellit —
    nōn ille amīcī fāta lūg___ aut frātr___;
    uter_____ nātus vīvat et prec___ vīvat;
    salva est et uxor sarci_____que ser___que;
    n___il colōnus vīlicus_____ dēcoxit.
 10 Maerōr___ igitur causa quae? Dom___ cēnat.
                                                    Martial

First removal: unit 10

R37 Mī__ris veter__, Vacerra, sōlōs
nec laudās ni__ mortuōs poēt__.
Īgnōs__s petimus, Vacerra: tant__
nōn est, ut plac__m tibī, per__e.
Martial

R38 Nōn dō__m tibi c__ meōs libellōs
ōra__ī totiēns et exige__ī
mī__ris, Theodōr__? Magna causa est:
d__ēs tū mihi n__ tuōs libellōs.
Martial

R39 Scrībere mē qu__eris, Vēlōx, epigra__ata longa.
Ip__ nihil scrībis: tū brevi__a facis.
Martial

R40 Nūbere vīs Prīsc__. Nōn mīr__, Paula; sapī'stī.
Dūc__ tē nōn vult Prīscus, et ille sap__.
Martial

R41 Uxōr__ nōn vīs Pollam, nec Polla marī__
tē vult. Bunne, sap__, nec minus illa sap__.
John Parkhurst,
Bishop of Norwich (1512-1575)

R42 Qu__ convīvā__ sine mē tam saepe, Luperce,
invēnī noc__m quā rati__ tibī.
Īrāsc__. Licet ūsque vocēs mitt__que rogēsque —
"Quid fac__s?" inquis? Quid faciam? Ven__.
Martial

R43 Tū Sētīna qui__ semper vel Massica pōn__,
Pāpyle, sed rūmor t__ bona vīna neg__.
Dīce__ hāc factus caelebs quat__ esse lagōnā.
Nec putō ___ crēdō, Pāpyle, ___ sitiō.
Martial

UNIT 11

S45 Aud__, vidē, tac__, sī vīs vīvere in pāce. *Medieval*
S46 Bene fer__ magnam disc__ fortūnam. *Horace*
S47 Sī qu__ agis, prūdenter agās et respic__ fīnem. *Translation of Aesop*
S48 Dīvid__ et imper__. *Anonymous*

R44 Aegrōtās ūnō deci____ aut saep____ annō;
    nec ti__ sed nō____ hoc, Polycharme, nocet.
Nam quoti____ surgis, sōtēria poscis amīc__.
    S__ pudor: aegrō__ jam, Polycharme, semel.
                      Martial

R45 Nōn dē vī neque caede n__ ven____,
    sed līs est mi__ dē tri____ capellīs.
Vīcīnī quer__ hās ab____e fūrtō.
Hoc jūdex s____ postulat prob____.
5 Tū Cann__ Mithridāticumque bell__
    et perjūr__ Pūnicī furōr__
et Sull__ Mariōsque Mūcī__que
    mag__ vōce son__ manūque tōtā.
Jam d__, Postume, dē tribus capel____.
                      Martial

R46 C__ mē capt____s, mittēbās mūnera nōbīs.
    Postquam cēp____ī, dās mihi, Rūfe, n____l.
Ut captum ten__s, captō quoque mūnera mit__,
    dē caveā fug__t nē male pā__us aper.
                      Martial

First removal: unit 12

R47 **Lup___ et agn___**

    Ad rīvum e___dem lupus et agnus vēn___nt
    sit_ compulsī. Super____ stābat lupus,
    lo____que īnferior agnus. Tu___ fauce improbā
    latrō incitātus jūrg___ causam in____it.
5 "Cūr" inquit "turbulent___ fēcistī m____
    aquam bib____ī?" Lāniger contrā ti___ns:
    "Q___ possum, quaesō, facere quod quere____, lupe?
    Ā tē dēcurrit ad meōs haust___ liqu___."
    Repulsus ille vēritā____ vīr____,
10 "Ante hōs sex mēns___ male" ait "d___istī mihī."
    Respondit agnus: "Equid___ nātus nōn er___."
    "Pater, Hercle, tuus" ille inquit "ma___ dīxit mi___."
    Atque ita cor____tum lacer___ injūstā nece.
    Haec propter ill___ scrīpta est homin___ fābula
15 quī fict___ causīs innocent___ opprimunt.
                                     Phaedrus

UNIT 12

S49 Ēn ego Fortūna! S_ st___em sorte sub ūnā
    et nōn mūt___er, numquam "Fortūna" voc___er.
                                     Medieval

S50 Sī qu___ barbātum fac___et sua barba beātum,
    in mundī circō nōn e___et sānct___ hircō.
                                     Medieval

S51 Sī fo___t in terrīs, rīd___et Dēmocritus. *Horace*

R48 Nūb___ Paula cupit nōbīs; ego dūc___ Paulam
    nōlō: anus est. Vel___m, sī mag___ esset anus.
                                     Martial

R49 **Vul____ et corv____**

Quī sē laud____ gau__t verbīs subdolīs,
fer__ dat poenās tur__ paenitentiā.

Cum dē fenestrā co_____ rap_____ cāseum
com__se vel__t, celsā residēns arbore,
5 vulpēs invīdit; de__de sīc coepit lo_____:
"Ō quī tuārum, corv__, penn_____ est nitor!
Quantum decor__ corpore et vultū ger__!
Sī vōcem hab__ēs, nūlla prior āles fo__t!"
At ille stult__, dum vult vōcem ostend_____,
10 lātō ōre ēmīsit cāse____, qu__ celeriter
dol__a vulpēs avidīs rapuit dent_____.
Tum dēmu__ ingemuit cor__ dēceptus stupor.
Phaedrus

R50 **Va__a, cape__a, ovis, et leō**

Numquam est fidēlis cum pote__e socie____:
testā_____ haec fābella prō_____itum meum.

Vacca et capella et patiē__ ovis injūri__
sociī fu__e cum leōne in salt_____.
5 Hī c__ cēp_____ent cervum vastī corporis,
sīc est locūtus, part_____ fact__, leō:
"Ego prīm__m tollō, nōmin__ quoniam 'Leō.'
Secundam, quia sum fortis, tribu__is mi__.
Tum qu__ plū__ valeō, mē sequētur tertia.
10 Malō affic____tur, sī qu__ quārtam tetigerit."
Sīc tōt__ praedam sōla improbi_____ abstulit.
Phaedrus

First removal: unit 13

R51 **Vulp___ et cap___**

Homō in perīc'l___ sim___ ac vēnit callidus,
reper____ effugium quaerit alter____ malō.

C___ dēcidi___et vulpēs in puteum īnscia
et alti___e claude___tur margine,
5 dēvēnit hirc___ sitiēns in eu___em locum.
Sim___ rogāvit e___et an dulcis liquor
et cōpi___us, illa fraudem mōli___s:
"Dēscen___, amīce! Tanta bonitās est aqu___
voluptās ut satiā___ nōn pos___t mea."
10 Immīsit sē barb____s. T___ vulpēcula
ēvāsit puteō, nī___a celsīs corn____,
hirc___que clausō līquit haerent___ vadō.
Phaedrus

UNIT 13

S52 Morit___ī tē salūt___us. *Based on Suetonius*

R52 **A___s ad amphor___**

Anus jac___e vīdit ēpōt___ amphoram,
adh___c Falernā faece ē testā nōbi___
odōr___ quae jūcundum lātē sparg___et.
Hunc postquam tōt___ avida trāxit nāri___:
5 "Ō suāvis anima! Quāl___ in tē dī___m bonum
anteh___c fui___e, tālēs cum sint reliquiae?"

Hoc qu___ pertin___t dīcet quī mē nōverit.
Phaedrus

R53 Īnscrīpsit tumul___ septem scelerāta vir____
        sē fēc____e Chloē. Quid po___ simplicius?
Martial

R54   Jactat inaequālem Matho m__ fēc____e libellum.
         Si vērum est, l__dat car____a nostra Mathō.
      Aequāl_ __. scrībit librōs Calvīn____ et Umber:
         aequāl___ liber est, Crētice, quī mal__ est.
                                                          Martial

R55   **Lupus et vulpēs, jūdi___ sī___ō**

      Quīcumque turp__ fraud__ semel innōtuit,
      etiam sī vērum dīcit, ā____tit fid___.
      Hocc at____tātur brevis Aesōp__ fābula.

      Lupus arguēbat vulpem fūr___ crīm____;
   5 negābat illa sē esse culp__ proxim___.
      Tu__ jūdex inter ill___ sēdit sīmius.
      Uter____ causam cum perōrā' ____ent suam,
      dīx____e f___tur sīmius sententiam:
      "Tū nōn vid____s perdid___e quod petis;
  10 tē crēdō sur____uisse quod pulch__ negās."
                                                         Phaedrus

R56   **Rā____ ad s__em**

      Vīcīnī fūr__ celebrēs vīdit nūpti___
      Aesōpus et continu__ nārrāre c__pit:
      "Uxōrem qu__dam Sōl cum ve__et dūcere,
      clāmōrem rānae sustul____ ad sīd____.
   5 Convīc___ permōtus quaerit J_____r
      causam querē____. Quaed___ tum stāgnī incola
      'Nunc' inquit 'omn___ ūnus exūrit lac___
      cōgitque miser___ āridā sēde ēmo___.
      Quidn__ futūrum est, sī creā'____ līberōs?' "
                                                         Phaedrus

UNIT 14

S53   Vigilā___ et ōrā___. *Anonymous*
S54   Quaeri___ Dominum, et vīv__t anima vestra. *Anonymous*
S55   Dum Fāta sin____, vīv__e laetī. *Seneca*

R57 Aqu____, fēl__ et aper

Aquila in sub__mī quercū nīdum fēc__at;
f__ēs cavernam nac__ in mediā pepererat;
sūs, nemor__ cultrīx, fētum ad īmam po__erat.
Tum fortuitum fēlē_ contubern____
5 fraude et scelest_ sīc ēvertit malitī_.
Ad nīd__ scandit volucr____. "Perniciēs" ait
"tibī parātur, fors__ et miser__ mihī!
Nam, fod__e terram quod vidēs cottī____
aprum īnsid____um, qu____um vult ēvertere,
10 ut nostr__ in plānō facile prōgeni____ opprimat."
Terrōre offūsō et perturbā____ sēns____,
dērēpit ad cub__ saetōs__ suis.
"Magn_" inquit "in perīc'lō sunt nā__ tuī.
Nam, sim__ exi__is pāstum cum tenerō grege,
15 aquila est parā__ rapere porc__lōs tibī."
H__c quoque timōre post____ complēvit locum,
dolōsa tūtō condidit sē__ cav_.
In__ ēvagāta noctū suspēn__ pede;
ubi ēs__ sē replēvit et prōl__ suam,
20 pav__em sim__āns prōspicit tōtō diē.
Ruīn__ metuēns aquila rām__ dēsidet;
aper rapī____ vītāns nōn prōdit for__.
Qu__ multa? Inediā sunt cōnsūmptī cum su__
fēl__que catulīs lārgam praebuērunt dap__.

25 Quantum homo bilinqu__ saepe concinn__ malī
documentum habēre h__nc stulta crēdulī____ potest.
Phaedrus

R58 Cani_ fidēl__

Repe____ līberālis stultīs grāt__ est;
vēr__ perītīs irrit__ tendit dolōs.
No__urnus cum fūr pānem mīs__et canī,
objec__ temptāns an ci__ posset capī,
5 "Heus!" inquit "lingu__ vīs meam praeclūd____,
n_ lātr__ prō rē dominī? Multum falleris.
Namque ista subita mē jub__ ben__itās
vigil____, faci__ nē meā culpā lucrum."
Phaedrus

R59 Nīl mihi dās vīvus; dīcis post fā___ dat___um.
      Sī nōn es stul___, scīs, Maro, qu___ cupiam.
                                              Martial

R60 Ā fēminīs utcumque spoli___ vir___
      (am___nt, ame___) nempe exemplīs discimus.

      Aetāt___ medi___ quendam mulier nōn rudis
      tenēbat (ann___ cēlāns ēlegan___)
    5 anim___que ejusdem pulchra juv___ cēperat.
      Amb___, vidērī dum volunt illī par___,
      capillōs hom___ legere coep___ in vicem.
      Quī sē put___et fing___ cūrā mulierum
      calvus rep___e factus est. Nam fundi___
   10 cān___ puella, nigr___ anus ēvellerat.
                                              Phaedrus

R61 Quod lānā cap___t allig___, Charīne,
      nōn aurēs ti___ sed dolent capi___.
                                              Martial

UNIT 15

R62 S___or et fr___er

      Praecep___ monitus saepe tē cōnsīder___.

      Habēbat quīd___ fīliam turpi___imam
      īdemque īns___nem pulchrā fac___ fīlium.
      Hī speculum, in cathedrā mātr___ ___t positum fuit,
    5 puerīli___ lūdentēs for___ īnspexērunt
      Hic sē form___um jactat; illa īr___citur
      ne___ glōriant___ sustinet frātris jocōs,
      accipiēns (Qu___enim?) cūncta in contumēli___.
      Ergo ad patrem dēcurrit laes___a in vic___
   10 magnāque invid___ crīminā___ fīlium.
      vir nātus quod rem fēminā___ tetig___it.
      Amplex___ ille utr___que et carpēns ōscula
      dulc___que in ambōs cāritātem part___ns:
      "Cottīd___" inquit "speculō vōs ūt___ volō:
   15 tū form___ nē corrumpās nēquiti___ malīs;
      tū faci___ ut istam mōribus vin___s bonīs."
                                              Phaedrus

First removal: unit 15

R63   C____us ad font____

Laudātīs ūtil____ra quae contemps____īs
saepe invenī____ te____is haec nārrātiō est.

Ad font____ cervus, cum bibi____et, restitit
et in liqu_____ vīdit effigiem su____.
5 Ibi dum rām____a mīrāns laudat cor____a
crūr____que nimiam tenuit____em vituperat,
vēnant____ subitō vōci_____ conterritus
per campum fug_____ coepit et cursū lev____
canēs ēlū____t. Silva tum excēpit fer____,
10 in quā retent____ impedītus corni_____
lacerā_____ coepit morsi_____ saevīs canum.
Tunc mor____ns ēdidi____e vōcem hanc dīcitur:
"Ō mē īnfēlīc____! Quī nunc dēm____ intellegō
ūtilia mihī quam fu____int quae dēspex____am
15 et quae laud__'ram, quantum lūct____ habuerint."
                                            Phaedrus

R64   Leō senex, aper, t____us, et as_____

Quī_____que āmīsit dīgni____tem prīstinam,
īgnāv____ etiam jocus est in cās__ gravī.

Dēfe____us annīs et dēsertus vīri_____
leō c____ jacēret spīritum extrēmum trahē____,
5 aper fulmine____ spūmāns vēnit dent_____
et vindic____it ict__ veterem injūriam.
Īnfēstīs taurus mo__ cōn____dit cornibus
hostīl__ corpus. Asinus, ut vīd__t ferum
im____ne laedī, calcibus frontem ext____it.
10 At il____ exspīrāns: "Fort____ indīgnē tulī
mi____ īnsultāre; tē, nātūr____ dēdecus,
quod ferre cōg____, certē bis videor mor____."
                                            Phaedrus

R65 **Equ__ et ap__**

    Equus sēdā__ solitus quō fuerat sit__,
    dum s__ē aper volūtat tur__vit vadum.
    Hin__ orta līs est. Sonip__ īrātus ferō
    auxilium peti'it homin__. Qu__ dorsō levāns
5 rediit ad hostem laet__. Hu__c tēlīs eques
    post_____ interfēcit, sīc locūtus tr__itur:
    "Laetor tuli__e auxilium mē prec_____ tuīs.
    Nam pr__dam cēpī et d__icī quam sīs ūtilis."
    Atq__ ita coēgit frēnōs invītum pat__.
10 Tum maestus __le: "Parvae vindict__ reī
    d__ quaerō dēmēns, servitūtem rep__erī."

    Haec īrācund__ admonē__t fābula
    i__ūne potius laedī qu__ dēdī alterī.
                                      Phaedrus

UNIT 16

S56 Sī tacu__sēs, philosophus mānsis_____. *Attributed to Boethius*
S57 Hectora quis nō'__et, sī fēlīx Troja f__set? *Ovid*
S58 Ō fīl__ cāre, nō__ nimis altē volāre. *Medieval*
S59 __lī mē tang__e. *John*
S60 N__ī barbam velle__ mortuō leōnī. *Martial*
S61 Contrā verbōsōs n_____ contend__e verbīs. *Dionysius Cato*

First removal: unit 16

R66 A___us et leō vēna___ēs

  Virtūt__ expers, verbīs j__tāns glōriam,
  īgnōt__ fallit, nōt__ est dērīsuī.

  Vēnā__, asellō comite, cum ve__et leō,
  contēxit illum frut__e et admonuit s__ul
5 ut īnsu__ā vōce terr__et ferās,
  fugientēs ip__ excip__et. Hīc aurītulus
  clāmōrem subi__ tollit tōtīs vīr_____
  nov_que turbat bēstiās mīrāc___.
  Qu__, dum paventēs exitūs nōtōs pet__t,
10 leō___ afflīguntur horrendō impe___.
  Quī, postquam cae__ f__sus est, asinum ēvocat
  jubetque vōcem preme___. Tunc ille īns__ēns:
  "__ālis vidētur opera tibī vōc__ meae?"
  "Īnsīgnis" inquit "sī_ ut, nisi nō'__em tuum
15 animum gen__que, similī fūg__sem metū."
                                  Phaedrus

R67 Quid Deus intend__, nōlī perquī___e sorte;
  qu__ statuat dē tē, si_ tē dēlīberat ille.
                                  Dionysius Cato

R68 Mustēl_ __ homō

  Mustēla ab hom___ prēnsa, cum īnstant__ necem
  effugere v__let, "Parce, quae__," inquit "mihī,
  quae ti_ mol__tīs mūribus pūrgō domum."
  Respondit ille, "Fa__rēs sī causā m__,
5 grātum es__t et de__ssem veniam supplicī;
  Nunc, quia labōrās ut fru__is reliqui__
  quās sunt rōs__ī, si_l et ipsōs dēvorēs,
  nōlī imputā__ vānum beneficium mi__."
  Atque ita locū__s improbam lēt_ dedit.

10 Hoc in s_ dictum dēbent illī agnō__ere,
  quōrum prīvāta s__vit ūtilitās si_,
  et meritum inā__ jactant imprūdent____.
                                  Phaedrus

R69 Quisquis Flāmini___ teri__, viātor,
        nōlī nōbile praeter___e marm___.
        Urb___ dēliciae salēsque Nīl__,
        ars et grātia, l___us et volup___s,
     5 Rōmānī de___s et dolor theāt___
        atque omnēs Vener___ Cupīdin___que
        hōc sunt cond___a qu__ Paris sepulchrō.
                                    Martial

R70 Cum tua nōn ē___s, ca___is mea carmina, Laelī.
        Carpe___ vel nōlī nostra vel ēd___ tua.
                                    Martial

R71 Ūndec___ns ūnā surrēx'tī, Zōile, cē___,
        et mūt___a tibi est synthesis ūn___iēns,
        sūdor inhaer___et madidā n__ veste retentus
        et lax___ tenuis laeder___ aura cutem.
     5 Quā rē ego nōn sū___, quī tēcum, Zōile, cē___?
        Frīg___ enim magnum synthesis ū___ facit.
                                    Martial

UNIT 17

S62 Carth___ dēle___a est. *Cato (adapted)*
S63 Pānis fīliōrum nōn objici___us can___. *Matthew*
S64 Dēlībera___m est saepe, stat___dum est semel. *Publilius Syrus*
S65 Diū appara___um est bellum, ut vincās celer___s. *Publilius Syrus*
S66 Vitium uxōris aut tolle___um aut fer___dum est. *Varro*

UNIT 18

S67 Dēlīber___ō disci____ sapientia. *Publilius Syrus*
S68 Dēlīber___ō saepe per__ occāsiō. *Publilius Syrus*
S69 Neg___ī causa avā__ numquam dēficit. *Publilius Syrus*
S70 Leg___ī semper occāsiō est, audi___ī nōn semper. *Pliny the Younger*
S71 Breve . . . tempus aetātis; satis est longum ad b___ honestēque vīv___um. *Cicero*
S72 Jūstitia est cōnstāns et perpetua voluntās jūs su__ cui__ tribuendī. *Justinian*
S73 Male imper___ō summ__ imperium āmittitur. *Publilius Syrus*

First removal: unit 21

R72 Nihil ... sine rati___ fac___dum est. *Seneca*
R73 Citō scrīb___dō fit ut bene scrīb___ur; bene scrībendō fit ut citō. *Quintilian*
R74 Sapientia ... ars vīv___dī put___da est. *Cicero*
R75 Ratiōne, nōn vī, vi___enda adul___entia est. *Publilius Syrus*
R76 Nihil a___ndō hominēs male agere di___nt. *Marcus Porcius Cato*

UNIT 19

S74 Nēmō est tam fortis quī_ reī novitāte perturb___. *Caesar*
S75 Nōn l___et in bellō bis pecc___e. *Anonymous*
S76 Semel in annō _ice_ īnsān___e. *Anonymous*
S77 Quod licet J___ nōn l___ bovī. *Anonymous*
S78 Ēsse oport___ ut vīvās, nōn vīv___e ut edās. *Anonymous*

UNIT 21

S79 Spectāt___ veniunt; veniunt spect___ur ut ipsae. *Ovid*

second removal

UNIT 1

S1 ____em nocēns verētur, ____tūnam ____nocēns. *Publilius Syrus*
S2 St_____ stult_ l_____tur. *Anonymous*
S3 Cr_____ntem ____quitur p_____iam cūra. *Horace*
S4 Nōn o____ēs eadem m____antur amant____. *Horace*
S5 A____rus, ni____ cum moritur, nīl r_____ facit. *Publilius Syrus*
S6 Ē v_____ r_____um vīpera nāscitur. *Anonymous*
S7 S_____itur superb____ f_____am. *Anonymous*
S8 C____ae l____ēs l____untur, ingentēs stupent. *Seneca*
S9 ____um sequitur lū____ semper innocen_____. *Publilius Syrus*
S10 Du____ quī sequitur l_____rēs neutrum c_____t. *Medieval*

S11   Qu____ dī dīligunt,
 adulēsc_____ moritur, d____ valet, sentit, sapit.
          Plautus

R1 Sē sōlum Labiēnus am____, mīr_____, adōr____:
 nōn m_____ s_ sōlum, sē quo_____ sōlus amat.
      Joannes Audoenus (Renaissance)

UNIT 2

S12 Cr____ō tē, Aeacidā, R_____ōs vinc____ posse. *Ennius*
S13 Ēv____us doc____ fortēs Fortūnam j____āre. *Livy*

R2 Dīc____ a_____ tuī bell____ ardēre puellās,
 quī f_____m sub aq____, Sexte, n_____ntis habēs.
          Martial

Second removal: unit 3

R3 D____ form__am, dīcis tē, B____, puellam.
    ____tud, qu__ nōn est, dīc____, Bassa, solet.
    Martial

R4 Versi____ōs in mē n____ātur scr____ Cinna.
    Nōn ____it, ____ carmina n__ legit.
    Martial

R5 M____ītur ____ tē viti__um, Zōile, dīcit.
    Nōn v____ōsus h__o es, Zōile, sed v____um.
    Martial

R6 O__us es et l__plēs et Brūtō c____ule nātus.
    Esse t____ vēr____ crēdis am____tiās?
    Sunt vēr__, sed quās juven__, quās paup__ habēbās.
    ____ novus est, mortem dīl____t ille t____.
    Martial

UNIT 3

S14 In pr____bium cessit sapientiam v____ ob____ārī. *Pliny*
S15 Nēmō ... ____ere potest n____ quī et r____. *Seneca*
S16 Et m__re et m____rī pr__um est vērae amīcitiae. *Cicero*
S17 Dulc__ et decōrum est prō pa____ ___rī. *Horace*
S18 Et ____ere et patī f____ia Rōmān__est. *Livy*
S19 Stultum est qu__ dē advers__ ubi culpa est ____. *Publilius Syrus*
S20 ____ līb____ās cecidit, audet līberē l____ nēmō. *Publilius Syrus*
S21 Ōre pl__ vel b____re v__ loquī nec honestum est nec tūtum. *Petrus Alphonsus*

R7 Fūnera p____ septem n__sit tibi Galla vir____,
    Pīcentīne. Sequī v__t, p__o, Galla ____ōs.
    Martial

R8 P____ vidērī Cinn_ v____. Et est pauper.
    Martial

UNIT 4

S22 E__mus, b____mus, gaudeāmus; post mortem nūlla vol____ās. *Anonymous*
S23 Rap_____, amīcī, oc_____nem dē d__. *Horace*
S24 __at jūst_____, ruat cael__. *Legal*
S25 Omnia v____it Amōr; et n__ cēdāmus Am____. *Vergil*
S26 Quī dēsīderat p__em praep_____ b___um. *Vegetius*
S27 Ferās, n__ culpēs, qu__ mūt____ nōn potest. *Publilius Syrus*
S28 Amēs p_____ntem, sī aequ__ est; sī ali____, ferās. *Publilius Syrus*
S29 Quī d___it b____ficium taceat; nārret quī ac____it. *Seneca*
S30 Aut b__at ___ a__at. *Cicero*

R9 O__ēs quās ____uit, Fabiāne, Lycōris amīc__
      ex____it. Ux____ fīat am____ meae.
                             Martial

UNIT 5

S31 Nōn ut e____ vīvō, sed __ vīvam ed_. *Quintilian*

R10 Cūr nōn mitt__ meōs t____, Pontiliāne, _____lōs?
      N__ mihi tū m_____s, Pontiliāne, __ōs.
                           Martial

R11 Ex__is ut nostrōs dōnem tibi, Tucc__, libell__.
      N__ faciam. N__ v__ vendere, nōn legere.
                           Martial

R12 Et jūdex p_____ et __ etit p_____nus.
      S_____s cēns___, Sext_, crēditōrī.
                           Martial

R13 Ex____s __ dōnem nostrōs tibi, Quīnte, l_____ōs.
      Nōn h____ō, sed h____t b_____opōla Tryphōn.
      "Aes da__ prō nūgīs et em__ tua carmina sān__?
      Nōn" inquis "faci__ tam f___ē." Nec e__.
                           Martial

R14 Semper agis c___ās et r__ agis, Attale, s___er.
      Est, nōn ____ quod agās, A_____, s_____ agis.
      Sī r__ et c___ae dēsunt, agis, Attale, mūl__.
      A_____, n_ quod agās dē____, agās animam.
                           Martial

Second removal: unit 6

R15 Sī m____ī, f____ant tibi qu____or, Aelia, dentēs.
      Exp__it ū__ d____ tussis et ūna duōs.
  Jam sēcūr__ potes tōt__ tussīre diē____:
      nīl i__īc qu__ agat tertia t____s habet.
Martial

UNIT 6

R16 Quid m____ r____at ager quaer____, Line, Nōmentānus?
      Hoc m____ r____it ager: tē, Line, nōn vid____.
Martial

R17 Nesc____ tam mult__ quid scrībās, Faust__, puellīs.
      H__ sc____, quod scrībit n____a puella tibī.
Martial

R18 ____tis Athēnagorās nōn m__it mūner__ nōbīs
      quae mediō brūm__ mitt____ mēn__ solet.
  __ sit Ath_____ trīstis, Faustīn__, vidēbō;
      m__ cert__ trīstem fēcit Ath_____.
Martial

R19 Scīs tē c____rī; scīs h__c, quī c____t, avārum;
      et __īs quī c____t quid, Mariāne, v____.
  Tū tamen hunc tabulīs hērēd__, stult__, su____īs
      scrīb__ et esse tuō vīs, f____se, loc__.
5 "Mūn____ magna tamen m____." S__ mīsit in hāmō.
      E__ piscātōrem pisc__ amāre pot____?
  Hiccī__ dēflēbit vē__ tua fāta dolō__?
      S__ cup__ ut plōret, dēs, Mariāne, n____.
Martial

R20 ____ō Philaenis semper a____ō pl____t.
    ____ fīat istud quaeritis m____? L__ca est.
Martial

R21 Dē___mās bellē, c___ās agis, Attice, b___ē;
     h___iās bellās, c___na ___a facis;
     com___is bellē mīm___, epigramm___ bellē;
     bellus gramma_____, bellus _s astrol_____;
5   et ___ē cantās et salt___, Attice, ___ē;
     ___us es arte lyrae; ___us es arte pil___.
     Nīl bene c__ f_____, faciās t__n omnia bellē.
     Vīs dīc__ qu__ sīs? Magnus es ardal___.
                                        Martial

UNIT 7

R22 __ v___e et ū___

     Famē co___a v___ēs al__ in vīneā
     ū___ ap___ēbat, summīs s___ēns vīribus.
     Quam t___ere ut nōn potu___, dis___ēns ait,
     "Nōn___ mā___a es; nōlo a_____am sūmere."
5   Quī facere qu__ nōn pos_____, verbīs ēl___ant,
     āsc_____ere h__ dēbē_____t exemplum sibī.
                                       Phaedrus

R23 D_ v___is h___num

     Pērās im___uit J_____ter n_____ duās:
     pr___īs repl_____ vitiīs post t___um dedit;
     a___nīs ante p_____us susp___it gravem.
     Hāc rē vidēre n_____a mal_ nōn poss_____;
5   al__ _imu_ dēlinquunt, cēnsōrēs s___s.
                                       Phaedrus

R24 V_____s ad p_____am ___gicam

     _____ōnam _____icam fort_ vulpēs vīderat.
     "Ō qua___ speci___" inqu___ "cerebrum nōn habet!"
     H__ illīs dict__ est quibus honōrem et glōr_____
     F_____a tribu___, sēnsum commūn___ abstulit.
                                       Phaedrus

Second removal: unit 8

R25   Pass____ ____ leporem cōnsili_____

   Sibi nōn cav____ et ali____ cōnsilium d____
   stult____ esse p_____īs ostendāmus v____ibus.

   Op_____sum ab aquilā, flētūs et d____tem grav____,
   leporem obj____ābat p_____. "Ubī per____itās
5 nōt__" _____it "illa est? Qu____ ita ce____'runt pedēs?"
   D____ loqu_____, ipsum accipiter necopīnum r____it
   qu____tūque vānō clāmitant____ inter_____t.
   L_____s s_____animus: "Mortis ēn sōlāc_____!
   Quī m____ sēcūr____ nostra irrīdēbās m_____,
10 similī querēl__ f_____ dē_____rās tua."
                                                Phaedrus

UNIT 8

R26   Can____ per fluvi____ c_____em ferēns

   A_____tit meri____ proprium quī aliēn____ appetit.

   C_____s per flūmen carn____ cum f____ret natāns,
   l____phārum in spe____lō vīdit simul_____um suum,
   aliam_____ praedam ab al____rō ferrī p____āns,
5 ēr____ere voluit. Vēr____ dēc____ta aviditās,
   et quem tenē____t ōre dīm____it c____um,
   n__c quem petē_____ ade__ potuit tangere.
                                                Phaedrus

R27   **Mūlī d__ et lat__ēs**

   Mūlī gra__ī sar__īs ī__nt duo;
   ūn__ ferē__t fiscōs c__ pecūniā,
   alter tum__ēs mul__ saccōs horde__.
   Ille one__ dīves celsā cervīce ēmin__
5 clārumque coll__ j__tat tin__nābulum;
   come__ quiētō sequi__ et pla__ō gradū.
   Sub__ l__ōnēs ex īnsidiīs ad__ant;
   dī__iunt nummōs; neg__unt vīle horde__;
   in__que caedem ferrō mūlum sauci__.
10 Spol__tus igitur c__ūs cum flēret su__,
   "Equ__em" inquit alter "mē con__ptum gaud__;
   n__ nihil ām__ī n__c sum laesus vulnere."

   H__ argūmentō tūt__ est h__num tenuitās;
   magnae perīc'__ sunt op__ obnoxi__.
                              Phaedrus

UNIT 9

S32   Bon__ opīniō homin__ tū__ pecūniā est. *Publilius Syrus*
S33   Vī__ argentum est aur__, virtūtibus aur__. *Horace*
S34   Tant__ major fām__ sitis est quam virtūt__! *Juvenal*
S35   Int__rābilius nihil est __m fēmina dīv__. *Juvenal*
S36   Qu__ cl__ius a__rīs? *Motto*
S37   Sīm__ quam simil__ turpiss__ bēstia nōbīs! *Ennius*
S38   Multō grātius venit quod facil__ qu__ quod plē__ manū datur. *Seneca*

R28   **Rāna rup__ __ b__**

   Inops, po__ntem dum v__t imitārī, pe__t.

   In prāt__ qu__dam r__ cōnspexit bovem,
   et tā__a in__iā tant__ magnitūdinis
   rūg__am in__vit pellem. Tum nātōs su__
5 inter__āvit __n bove e__et lātior.
   Ill__ negā'runt. R__sus int__dit cutem
   maj__ nīsū, et simi__ quaesī__ modō
   quis ma__ e__et. Illī dīxērunt bo__.
   Novissimē in__nāta, d__ v__t validius
10 in__re sē__, ruptō jacuit cor__.
                              Phaedrus

Second removal: unit 9

R29 __ lapidem Torquātus habet prae__ia quārt__;
    ad quārtum, breve r__ ēm__ Octāci_____.
  Torquā____ nitidās var__ dē marm_____ thermās
    exs____xit; cucumam f__it Otāci_____.
5 D__posuit dāphnōna su__ Torquāt__ in agrō;
    castaneās cent__ sēv__ Otāci_____.
  Cōnsule Torquāt__, vīcī fuit il__ magis____;
    nōn minor in tan__ vī__s honōre s____.
  Gr__dis ut ex__uam bōs r_____m rūperat ōlim,
10   sī__, pu__, Torquātus rum____ Otācilium.
Martial

R30 Omnēs aut vet__ās ha__s a__cās
    aut turp__ ve__īsque f__diōrēs.
  H__ dūcis co__tēs trah__que tēcum
    p__ conv__ia, porticūs, th____ra.
5 S__ f__mōsa, Fabulla, sīc puella e__.
Martial

R31 Pet__ Gemell__ nū__iās Marōnillae
  et cup__ et īn__at et pr__ātur et dōnat.
  Aedō__ pulchra est? Im__, foedius n__ est;
  Qu__ ergō in illā petitur et pl__et? T_____.
Martial

R32 Septima j__, Philerōs, tibi cond_____ uxor in ag__.
  Plūs nūllī, Philerōs, qu__ t__ re__it ager.
Martial

R33 S____ bona, s____ quaedem mediocria, s____ mala plūra
  qu__ l__is hīc. Aliter nōn f__, Avīte, liber.
Martial

R34 Cast__ s__ glad__ cum trāderet Arria Paetō
    qu__ dē vīs_____ibus str__xerat ip__ suīs,
  (sī qu__ fidēs) "Vuln__ quod fēcī nōn dol__," inquit
    "sed tū qu__ faciēs, hoc m____, Paet__, dolet."
Martial

UNIT 10

S39 Fr__gar, n__ fle__ar. *Motto*
S40 Tr____mur omnēs stud__ l__dis. *Cicero*
S41 Vid__ meli____ probō____, dēteriōra sequor. *Ovid*
S42 Prōgredimur ____ō dūcit quem____ volun____. *Lucretius*
S43 Nāsc____ēs m__imur, fīnisque ab or__ine pendet. *Manilius*
S44 Temp____a mūtantur, nōs e__ m____mur in illīs. *Borbonius (?)*

R35 Rumpitur invidiā quī____, cārissim__ Jūl__,
    qu__ mē Rōma l__it; rumpitur inv____.
    Rum____ invidiā qu__ turbā se__r in omnī
    m____trāmur digi__; rumpi____ invidiā.
5 Rumpitur in____ trib____ quod C____ar uterque
    jūs mi__ nātōrum; r____r i____.
    ____r invidiā quod r__ mihi dulce sub ur__ est
    parva__ in urbe domus; ____ ____.
    Rumpitur invidiā ____d s__ jū__dus amīcīs,
10 q____ con__va fr____ēns; rumpitur invidiā.
    Rumpitur invidiā quod am____ q____que prob____.
    Rump____ qu__quis rumpitur ____.
                               Martial

R36 ____ fronte Seli__ nūbi__ vidēs, Rūfe,
    ____ ambulātor portic__ ter__ sēram,
    lūgu____ qu__dam ____ tacet piger vultus,
    ____ paene terr__ nās__ indecēns tangit,
5 ____ dextr__ pectus pulsat et com__ vellit
    nōn il__ amīc__ fā__ lūget aut frātris;
    u__rque nātus vīv__ et precor vīv__;
    sal__ est et uxor sarc__aeque s__vīque;
    nihil col__us vīl__usque d__oxit.
10 Maerōris ig__ur causa qu__? Do__ cēnat.
                               Martial

R37 Mīrāris v__erēs, Vacerr__, sō__s
    nec l__dās __si mort____ poētās.
    Ī____scās peti__s, Vacerra: t__tī
    nōn est, __t placeam t____, ____īre.
                              Martial

Second removal: unit 11

R38 N__ dōnem t___ cūr meōs libel___
     ōrant_ toti__s et exigent_
     mīrā___, Theodōre? M___a c__sa est:
     dōnēs tū mihi __ tu__ libell__.
                                        Martial

R39 Scrībere mē quer___s, Vēlōx, e__grammata l___a.
     __se nihil scrīb__: tū br__ōra facis.
                                        Martial

R40 Nūb__ v__ Prīscō. Nōn mīror, Paula; sapī'___.
     Dūcere tē nōn v__t Prīscus, et il__ s___t.
                                        Martial

R41 Ux__em nōn vīs Poll___, nec Poll_ marītum
     t_ vult. Bunne, s__is, nec mi___ illa sapit.
                                  John Parkhurst,
                        Bishop of Norwich (1512-1575)

R42 Quod conv__āris s___ mē t__ saepe, Luperce,
     inv__ī noceam quā r___ōne t___.
     Ī__scor. L__et ūsque voc__ mittāsque rogēsque —
     "Qu__ faciēs?" inqu__? Quid faci__? Veniam.
                                        Martial

R43 Tū Sētīna ___dem semper v__ Massica p__is,
     Pāpyl_, sed rūm__ __am bona vīna negat.
     D___ris h__ factus caelebs quater esse lagōn__.
     Nec pu__ nec crē__, Pāpyle, nec sit__.
                                        Martial

UNIT 11

S45 Audī, vi__, tacē, sī v__ vīvere in p___. *Medieval*
S46 B__e ferre magn__ disce fortū___. *Horace*
S47 __ quid agis, prūden___ ag__ et respice fīnem. *Translation of Aesop*
S48 Dī__de _t i__erā. *Anonymous*

R44 Aegrō___ ū__ deciēns aut saepius an___;
     _ec tibi sed nōbīs h__, Polycharme, n__et.
     N__ qu__ēns surgis, sōtēr__ poscis amīcōs.
     Sit pudor: aegrōtā j__, Polycharm_, sem__.
                                        Martial

R45   Nōn dē v__ neque cae__ nec v_____,
      sed l__ est mihi dē t__bus capel____.
      Vīcī__ qu__or hās abesse fūr__.
      H__ jūdex sibi po____lat pr____rī.
    5 T_ C__nās Mithridātī____que bellum
      et per____ria Pūni__ f__ōris
      et S__lās Mari____que Mūciōs____
      magnā vō__ s__ās ma__que tōtā.
      J__ dīc, Postum_, dē tr_____ capellīs.
                                              Martial

R46   Cum mē captārēs, mit_____ās mūn__a nōb__.
         Post_____ c__istī, dās mi__, Rūfe, nihil.
      _t captum teneās, cap__ qu__ue mūnera mitte,
         dē cav__ fugiat n__ male pāstus ap__.
                                              Martial

R47   **Lu____ e_ ag____**

      Ad rīv__ eun____ lupus et ____us vēnerant
      si__ compul__. Superior stābat l_____,
      longēque īnfer____ agnus. T_____ fauce im__obā
      latrō incit_____ jūrgiī caus__ intul__.
    5 "C__" inqu__ "turbulentam fēc____ī mihī
      aqu__ bibentī?" Lāniger cont__ t__ēns:
      "Q__ possum, quae__ō, facere quod qu__eris, lupe?
      Ā tē dēcur____ ad me__ haustūs l__uor."
      Repulsus il__ v_____tātis v__ibus,
   10 "An__ hōs __x mēnsēs male" a__ "dīxistī mihī."
      Resp____it agnus: "E____dem nāt__ nōn eram."
      "P_____r, Hercl__, tuus" ille inquit "male dīx__ mihī."
      Atque ita corrept__ l__erat inj__tā nece.

      Haec prop_____ illōs scrīp__ est hominēs fāb____
   15 quī f__tīs causīs in____entēs op_____munt.
                                              Phaedrus

UNIT 12

S49   Ēn ego Fortūna! Sī stā____ sor__ sub ū__
         et n__ mūt_____, numquam "Fortūna" voc_____.
                                              Medieval

Second removal: unit 12

S50 Sī quem barb____ faceret sua bar__ beāt___,
     in mun__ circō nōn es____ sānctior hirc_.
                                                        Medieval

S51 Sī f____t in terr__, rīd____ Dēmocritus. *Horace*

R48 Nūbere Paula c__it nō____; ego dūcere P_____
         nō__: a__s est. Vellem, sī magis es__t anus.
                                                        Martial

R49 V_____ e_ c__vus

     Quī s_ laudārī gaudet verb__ sub__līs,
     fe__ dat poe__s turpī paeni____tiā.

     C__ dē fene____ā corvus raptum cās____
     comēs__ vell__, celsā resid__s arbore,
   5 vulpēs in__dit; dein__ sīc c__pit loquī:
     "Ō qu_ tu____, corve, pennārum est ni____!
     Quant__ decoris corp____ et vul__ geris!
     S_ vōcem habē____, nūlla pri__ ālēs foret!"
     A_ il__ stultus, dum vult vōc__ ostendere,
  10 lātō ō_ ēm__it cāseum, quem celer_____
     d__ōsa vulpēs a__dīs r__uit dentibus.
     Tum dēm__ ing__uit corvī dēceptus stup__.
                                                        Phaedrus

R50 **Vacca, cape__a, o____, et l__**

     Numquam est fid__is cum potent__ so__tās:
     t____ātur haec fābe__a prōpositum me__.

     Va__a et ca__la et patiēns o__s injūriae
     s__iī fuēre cum le____ in s__tibus.
   5 Hī cum c__issent cerv__ vastī corp____,
     s__ est locū__, par__us factīs, leō:
     "Ego pr__am tol__, nōminor quo__am 'Leō.'
     Sec__dam, quia sum f__tis, tr__ētis mihī.
     Tum __ia p__s valeō, mē sequ_tur tertia.
  10 Ma__ afficiētur, sī __is quārtam tetig____t."
     Sīc tōtam praed__ sōla im_____itās ab__tulit.
                                                        Phaedrus

R51 **Vu____ e_ ca____**

Ho__ in perīc'lum simul a_ vēnit c____idus,
reperīre ef____ium quaerit al____ius mal__.

Cum dē____isset vulpēs in put____ īn____a
et alt____e cl____erētur marg____,
5 dēv__it hircus sit____ns in eundem loc__.
S__ul rogāvit esset a_ dulc__ liquor
et c__iōsus, illa fraud__ m__iēns:
"Dē__ende, amīce! Tan__ boni__ est aquae
volup____ ut s__iārī nōn p__sit mea."
10 Immīsit sē b____ātus. __um vulpēc__a
ēv__it put____, nīxa cels__ cornibus,
hircum____ clausō līqu__ h____entem vadō.
Phaedrus

UNIT 13

S52 M____tūrī t_ sal____mus. *Based on Suetonius*

R52 **____us a_ am____ram**

A____ jacēre vīd__ ē__tam amphoram,
ad__c Falern_ faece ē test__ nōbilī
odōrem quae jūcund____ lā__ sp____eret.
Hu__ post____ tōtīs avida tr__xit nāribus:
5 "Ō suāv____ anima! Quā__ in tē dīcam bon__
an__hāc fu__se, t__ēs cum sint reliquiae?"

Hoc ____ pertineat dīc__t quī mē nōv____t.
Phaedrus

R53 Īnscr____sit tum__īs septem scel____ta virōrum
s_ f____isse Chloē. Quid pote simplic____?
Martial

R54 Ja__at in__quālem Matho mē f____isse libellum.
Sī vēr____ est, laudat ____mina nos____ Mathō.
Ae____lēs scrībit libr____ Calvīnus __ Umber:
ae____lis liber est, Crētic__, quī __lus est.
Martial

Second removal: unit 14

R55 Lupus __ vulpēs, j_____e s____ō

Quī____que turpī fraude s__el inn__uit,
eti__ sī vērum d__it, āmittit f__em.
Hocc attest____r brevis Ae__pī f__ula.

Lupus ar__ēbat vulp__ f__tī crīmine;
5 ne__bat ill__ sē esse c__pae proximam.
__unc __dex int__ illōs sēdit sīmius.
Ut__que causam cum per____'ssent su__,
d__isse fer____ sīmius sent__iam:
"Tū nōn v____ēris er__disse quod p____s;
10 tē crēdō surripu____e quod p____rē n__ās."
Phaedrus

R56 ____ae a__ ____em

Vīc____ f__is celebrēs vīdit n__tiās
Aesōpus et cont____ō nārr__e coe____:
"Uxōrem quon____ Sōl cum vel__ dūc____,
clāmōrem rān__ sus____ēre ad sīd____.
5 Con__ciō permōt__ qu____it Juppiter
causam qu__ēlae. Qu__dam tum stāgnī in__la
'N__c' inquit 'omnēs ūnus ex__it __cūs
cōgit____ miserās āridā sē__ ē__rī.
Qu__nam fut__um est, sī cr__'rit līberōs?' "
Phaedrus

UNIT 14

S53 V____āte __t ō__te. *Anonymous*
S54 Q____rite Domin__, et vīvet ani__ vestra. *Anonymous*
S55 Du__ ā__ s____nt, vīvite laetī. *Seneca*

R57   **Aqu____, fē____, et ap____**

Aquila in sublīmī quer___ nīd___ fēc____t;
fēlēs cavern___ n___ta in mediā pe_____rat;
sū_, nemoris cultr____, fēt___ ad īmam posuerat.
Tu_ fortuit___ fēlēs cont_____rnium
5 frau___ et sce_____tā sīc ēvertit mal___iā.
Ad n___um sc___dit volucris. "Pernici___" ait
ti___ parātur, f_____an et miserae mi___!
N___, fodere terr___ qu_d vidēs cot___diē
apr___ īnsidiō_____, quercum vult ēvert_____,
10 _t nostram in plānō facile prō_____iem opprim_t."
Terr_____ offū___ et per____bātīs sēnsibus,
dēr___it ad cubīle saet___ae su___.
"Magnō" _____ "in per___'__ sunt nātī t___.
_am, s___ul exie_____ pāstum cum tenerō grege,
15 aquila est p_____ta r_____re porcellōs ti___."
Hunc quo_____ timōre p_____quam com_____vit locum,
dol_____ tūtō cond___it ___sē cavō.
Inde ēv_____ta noct_ suspēnsō pe___;
ubi ēscā ___ rep____it et pr___em suam,
20 pavōr___ simul___s prō_____cit tōtō diē.
R___nam metu_____ aquila rāmīs dē_____et;
aper rapīnam vīt___s nōn p___dit f___ās.
Quid mul___? Ined___ sunt cōns_____ tī cum suīs
fēlisque catul___ lār_____ praebu___unt dapem.

25 Quant___ homo bi_____guis saepe concinnet mal___
docu_____um hab_____ hi___ stulta crēdulitās potest.
                                                Phaedrus

R58   **C_____ f_____**

Re_____e līber_____s stult___ grātus est;
v_____m perī_____ irritōs tendit dol___.

Nocturnus cum f___ pā_____ mīsis_____ canī,
objectō temptā___ an cibō po___et cap_,
5 "He___!" inquit "linguam v___ me___ praeclūdere,
nē lātrem prō rē domi___? Mult___ falle_____.
N___que ista sub_____ m_ jubet benīgnitās
vig___āre, f___iās nē meā cul___ lucrum."
                                                Phaedrus

Second removal: unit 15

R59   Nīl m___ dās vīvus; dī__s p___ fāta datūrum.
      S_ nōn e_ stultus, scīs, Maro, quid cu__am.
                             Martial

R60   A fēm____ utc___ue sp___ārī virōs
     (a__nt, a__ntur) nem__ exemplīs discimus.

     Aetātis m___ae qu__dam mulier nōn rud__
     t__bat (annōs cēl___ ēl__ntiā)
5 animōs___ ejus___ pulchr_ juvenis cēperat.
     Ambae, vid__ dum vol__ il_ parēs,
     capill__ hominī legere c__pēre in vic__.
     Quī s_ putāret f__gī cūrā mulier__
     cal__ rep___ factus est. Nam f__itus
10 cānōs pu____, nigrōs a___ ēv__lerat.
                             Phaedrus

R61   Qu__ lā__ caput a_ligās, Charīne,
     nōn au__s t___ sed d__ent capillī.
                             Martial

UNIT 15

R62   ___or _t ____er

     Pr__ceptō moni___ saepe t_ cōnsīderā.

     Habē__t ___dam fīliam turpiss___m
     īd__que īnsīgn__ pulchrā faciē fīli__.
     H_ speculum, in cathe___ mātris ut posit__ fuit,
5 pu___liter lūde__ēs forte īnsp__ērunt.
     H_ sē formōsum jac__t; il_ īrāscitur
     nec gl__antis sustinet frātr__ j__ōs,
     ac__iēns (Quid e___?) cūn__a in contumēliam.
     Er__ ad patrem dēcurrit l___ūra in v__em
10 magnā___ invidiā crī__ātur fīl___,
     vir nā___ quod rem f__nārum t__igerit.
     Am__exus ille utrum___ et carpēns ōs__la
     dulcemque in amb__ cā___ātem pa__iēns:
     "C___īdiē" in___ "specul_ vōs ūtī volō:
15 t_ formam n_ corrump__ nēquitiae malīs;
     t_ faciem ut ist__ mōribus vinc__ bonīs."
                             Phaedrus

R63   C_____ a_ f____em

　　Laudāt__ ūt__iōra qu__ contempserīs
　　saepe in__īrī testis h__c nārrā____ est.

　　Ad fontem c__vus, c__ bibisset, rest__it
　　et in l____ōre vīdit ef____iem s__am.
5　Ib__ d__ rāmōsa mīrā__ laudat cornua
　　cr____umque n__iam te____tātem vituperat,
　　vēna____um subi__ vōcibus conterrit__
　　per camp__ fugere coep__ et cur__ levī
　　c__ēs ēlūsit. Silva t__ excē__t ferum,
10　in quā re__ntīs imp__ītus c__nibus
　　l__erārī c__pit morsibus saev__ canum.
　　Tu__ m__iēns ēd__isse vōcem hanc dīcitur:
　　"Ō m__ īnfēlīcem! Quī nunc d__um intel_gō
　　ūt__ia mihī qu__ fuer__t quae dēspexeram
15　et qu__ laudā'ram, quan__m lūctūs habu__int."
　　　　　　　　　　　　　　　　　　　Phaedrus

R64   Leō sen__, a____, taurus, et __inus

　　____cumque āmīsit dignitāt__ prīstin__,
　　īgn__īs et__m j__us est in cāsū gravī.

　　Dēfect__ a__īs et dēsert__ vīribus
　　leō cum jacē__t spīri____ ex__ēmum trahēns,
5　aper fulm__eīs spūmā__ vēnit d____ibus
　　et vindicāvit i__ū veter__ injūri__.
　　Īnfēst__ taurus m__x cōnfōdit corni__
　　host__e corp__. Asinus, _t vīdit ferum
　　impū__ laed_, calc____ frontem extūdit.
10　At i__e exspī__ns: "Fortīs ind__nē tulī
　　mihī īnsult__e; _ē, nātūrae dēde__s,
　　qu__ fer__ cōgor, certē b__ videor morī."
　　　　　　　　　　　　　　　　　　　Phaedrus

Second removal: unit 16

R65 E____ __ ap__

    Equus sēdāre s__itus qu_ fuerat s__im,
    d__ sēsē aper volū__t turbāvit v__um.
    H__c orta l__ est. Sonipēs īrātus fer_
    auxi_____ peti'it h____nis. Quem dors_ levāns
5 rediit ad h__tem laetus. Hunc tēl__ equ_s
    p____quam interf___it, sīc locū__s trāditur:
    "Laet__ t__isse auxilium mē precibus tu__.
    N_m praedam cēp_ et didi__ quam sīs ūtilis."
    Atque ita coēgit frēn__ invīt__ p__ī.
10 Tum mae__us ille: "Parv__ vindictam re_
    dum quaer_ dēmēns, servi__tem repper__."

    H__c ī__cundōs admonēbit fāb__a
    imp____ pot____ laedī quam dēd_ alterī.
                              Phaedrus

UNIT 16

S56 Sī ta__ssēs, philosoph__ m__sissēs. *Attributed to Boethius*
S57 Hecto__ quis n_'_set, sī fēlīx Troja fu___et? *Ovid*
S58 Ō fīlī cār_, n___ ni__s altē volāre. *Medieval*
S59 N__ m_ t__gere. *John*
S60 __lī barbam vellere mortu_ leōn_. *Martial*
S61 Contrā verb__ōs __ī cont__dere verbīs. *Dionysius Cato*

R66   A_____ et l__ ven___ēs

   Virt__is exp__s, verb__ jactāns glōriam,
   īgnōtōs fa__it, nōt__ est dērīs__.

   Vē____ī, asellō comi____, cum v__let leō,
   con__xit ill__ frutice et adm__uit simul
5 __t īnsuētā vō__ te__ēret ferās,
   fugi____ēs ipse exc__ret. Hīc aurī____us
   clāmōr__ subitō toll__ tō____ vīribus
   novōq__ turbat bē__iās mī____ulō.
   Quae, d__ pavent__ exit__ nōtōs petunt,
10 le____s afflīgu__ur hor__dō impetū.
   Quī, post____m c__e fessus est, asinum ēv__at
   j__tque vōc__ premere. Tu__ ille īnsolēns:
   "Quā____ vidētur ope__ t____ vōcis meae?"
   "In____nis" inquit "sīc ut, ni__ nō'ssem tu__
15 animum genusque, simi__ fū__sem met__."
                              Phaedrus

R67   Qu__ Deus intendat, n____ perquīrere sor__;
   __id stat____ dē tē, sine tē dēl__rat ille.
                              Dionysius Cato

R68   M__tēla e_ ho__

   Mustēla ab homine pr____a, c__ īnstantem ne__m
   effug____ vellet, "Pa__e, quaeso," inquit "mi__,
   __ae tibi molest__ mūr____ pūrgō domum."
   Respondit ille, "Face__s s_ cau__ meā,
5 grāt__ esset et dedis____ veniam suppli__.
   Nunc, quia labōr__ __t fr__ris reliquiīs
   qu__ sunt rōsūrī, simul et i__ōs dēvo__s,
   n__ī imputāre vān__ bene__cium mihī."
   At____ ita locūtus improb__ lē__ dedit.

10 H__ in sē dictum dē__nt illī agnōsc__e,
   qu__um prīv__a servit ūtil__ās sibī,
   et merit__ ināne jac__nt im____dentibus.
                              Phaedrus

Second removal: unit 19

R70 C__ t__ nōn ēdās, carpis mea carm____, Laelī.
   Carpere v__ n____ nostra v__ ēde tua.
                                                        Martial

R71 Ū.____ciēns ūnā surr__'tī, Zōil__, cēnā,
   et mūtāta ti__ est syn____sis ūndeci____,
   sūd__ inhaerēret mad____ nē veste retent__
   et l__am tenu__ laederet aur__ cutem.
 5 Quā rē e__ nōn ____dō, qu__ tēcum, Zōile, cēnō?
   Fr__us en__ magnum synthe____ ūna facit.
                                                        Martial

UNIT 17

S62 C____āgō dēl____ es__. *Cato (adapted)*
S63 P____s fīli____ nōn obj____endus canibus. *Matthew*
S64 Dēlīberan____ est saepe, st____ndum est s__el. *Publilius Syrus*
S65 Diū apparand__ est bellum, ut vinc__ c____ius. *Publilius Syrus*
S66 Vitium uxōr__ aut t____endum aut f____endum est. *Varro*

UNIT 18

S67 Dēlīberan__ di____tur sapie____a. *Publilius Syrus*
S68 Dēlīberan__ saepe p____t o__cāsiō. *Publilius Syrus*
S69 Negan__ causa a____ō numquam dēf____t. *Publilius Syrus*
S70 Legen__ semper occāsiō est, audien__ nōn s____er. *Pliny the Younger*
S71 Brev__ . . . tempus aetātis; s__is est longum ad bene honestēque vīven____. *Cicero*
S72 Jūstitia est cōnstāns et perpetua voluntās jūs s__m c____que tribue____. *Justinian*
S73 Mal__ imperan__ summum imperium āmitt____. *Publilius Syrus*

R72 N____l . . . s__ ratiōne f____ndum est. *Seneca*
R73 Citō scrībendō nōn f__ ut bene scrībātur; bene scr____ fit ut c____. *Quintilian*
R74 Sap____tia . . . ars v____ndī putan__ est. *Cicero*
R75 R____ōne, nōn __ vinc____a adulēscentia est. *Publilius Syrus*
R76 Nihil ag____ ho____ēs male ag____ discunt. *Marcus Porcius Cato*

UNIT 19

S74 Nēmō est t__ fortis qu__ r___ novitāte perturbētur. *Caesar*
S75 Nōn licet in be__ō b__ pe__āre. *Anonymous*

S76 S___l in annō l_____ īns__īre. *Anonymous*
S77 Qu__ l_____ Jovī nōn licet b____. *Anonymous*
S78 Ē_se o____tet ut vīvās, nōn vīvere ut ed__. *Anonymous*

UNIT 21

S79 Spect_____ veniunt; ven_____ spectentur ut ipsae. *Ovid*

third removal

UNIT 1

S1 Lēgem n____ns v____tur, F_____ innocēns. *Publilius Syrus*
S2 ____tus ____ta ____itur. *Anonymous*
S3 Crē____ntem sequitur p_____am c____. *Horace*
S4 Nōn omn____ ea____ mīra____t amantque. *Horace*
S5 Avārus, nisī ____ moritur, n____ rēctē ____t. *Publilius Syrus*
S6 Ē vīperā rurs____ v_____a n____itur. *Anonymous*
S7 S____tur ____bia ____mam. *Anonymous*
S8 Cūrae l____s loquuntur, ing____ēs ____pent. *Seneca*
S9 Suum sequitur ____en s____er ____ocentia. *Publilius Syrus*
S10 Duōs ____ sequitur leporēs ____trum ____it. *Medieval*

S11   Quem dī dīligunt,
    adulēscēns moritur, dum v____t, se____it, s____it.
                                Plautus

R1 ____ sōlum Labiēnus am____, mīrātur, a____rat:
      nōn modo ____ sōlum, ____ quoque sōlus ____t.
                Joannes Audoenus (Renaissance)

UNIT 2

S12 Crēdō tē, Aeacid____, Rōmān____ vincere ____se. *Ennius*
S13 Ēventus ____cuit f_____ F_____ juvāre. *Livy*

R2 Dīcis amōre t____ ____llās a____re puellās,
      ____ faciem sub _____, Sext____, natantis habēs.
                                Martial

R3 Dīcis ____ōsam, dīcis ___, Bassa, p_____.
     I___d, quae nōn est, ____ere, Bassa, s___t.
                                    Martial

R4 V_____culōs in ___ nārrātur ____ībere Cinna.
     ___ scrībit, cujus c_____ nēmo l___t.
                                    Martial

R5 Mentītur quī ___ vitiōsum, ____e, d____t.
     ___ vitiōsus homo ___, Zōil__, sed vitium.
                                    Martial

R6 Orbus ___ et locuplēs et Br____ cōnsule nāt___.
     ___se tibī vērās crē____ am_____s?
     S___ ____ae, sed quās juvenis, quās ____per habēbās.
     Quī novus ___t, m___.em dīligit il___ tuam.
                                    Martial

UNIT 3

S14 In prō_____ c___it _____tiam vīnō obumbrārī. *Pliny*
S15 N____ ... regere ____est nisī ___ et regī. *Seneca*
S16 Et monēre ___ monērī propri___ est v_____ amīcitiae. *Cicero*
S17 Dulc__ et decōr___ est ____ patriā morī. *Horace*
S18 ___ facere ___ patī fortia _____num est. *Livy*
S19 Stultum est querī ___ adversīs ____ c___a est tua. *Publilius Syrus*
S20 Ubī lībertās c____it, a___et līberē l_____ nēmō. *Publilius Syrus*
S21 Ō___ plēnō ____ bibere vel loquī n___ honestum est nec tūtum. *Petrus Alphonsus*

R7 F____ra ____ septem nūpsit ____i Galla virōrum,
     Pīcentīn__ . S____ vult, puto, ____a virōs.
                                    Martial

R8 Pauper v____rī Cinna ____t. Et ___ pauper.
                                    Martial

UNIT 4

S22 Edāmus, b_____, gaudeāmus; _____ mortem nūl__ voluptās. *Anonymous*
S23 ____iāmus, amī__, occāsiōnem ___ diē. *Horace*
S24 Fīat _____itia, __at c____um. *Legal*
S25 Om____ vincit ____ōr; et nōs c____mus Amōrī. *Virgil*
S26 ____ d____erat pācem pr____aret bellum. *Vegetius*
S27 F____s, nōn c____s, quod mūtārī nōn p___est. *Publilius Syrus*
S28 A___s parentem, ___ aequus est; sī aliter, f____s. *Publilius Syrus*
S29 ____ dedit beneficium t____t; nārret ____ accēpit. *Seneca*
S30 ____ bibat ____ ab__t. *Cicero*

R9 Omnēs quās hab__it, Fabiān__, Lycōris a_____
     ____tulit. Uxōrī ____t a____ meae.
                              Martial

UNIT 5

S31 Nōn ___ edam vīvō, sed ___ vīvam ___ō. *Quintilian*

R10 ____ nōn _____o meōs tibi, Pontiliān__, libellōs?
      ___ mihi t__ mittās, Pontiliāne, t____.
                              Martial

R11 Exig___ ut n____ōs dōnem tibi, Tucca, l_____ōs.
      Nōn ____iam. Nam vīs v____ere, nōn l____ere.
                              Martial

R12 Et j____ petit et _____ p_____.
      S_____ c____eo, Sexte, cr____tōrī.
                              Martial

R13 Exigis ut ____em n_____ōs tibi, Quīnt__, libellōs.
      Nōn ____eō, s__ ____et bibliopōla Tryphōn.
      "A__ dabō ____ nūgīs et emam tua c_____ sānus?
      ____" inquis "faciam t__ fatuē." N__ egō.
                              Martial

R14 S_____ ___is causās et rēs agis, Attale, s_____.
      Est, nōn est quod a___s, Attale, s_____ a___s.
      Sī rēs et causae dē___nt, ___is, Attale, ____ās.
      _____e, nē quod ___ās dēsit, ___ās animam.
                              Martial

R15 __ meminī, fuerant ___i quattuor, Aelia, ____ēs.
      Expulit ūna duōs t___is et ___ ____.
      Jam s____a __tes tōtīs _____īre diēbus:
        nīl i_____ quod ___t t____a tussis habet.
                                            Martial

UNIT 6

R16 _____ mihi r____t ager qu___is, Line, Nōmentānus?
       Hoc mihi reddit a___: __ L___, nōn videō.
                                            Martial

R17 Nescio t__ multīs quid s____ās, Fauste, _____īs.
       Hoc ___o, quod s____it nūlla puella t___.
                                            Martial

R18 Trīstis Athēnagorās ___ mīsit m___ra __bīs
      qu__ m___ō brūmae mittere m___e solet.
      __ __t Athēnagorās trīs____, Faustīne, vidēbō;
       mē cer__ tr_____ f___t Athēnagorās.
                                            Martial

R19   ___s __ captārī; ___s hunc, quī captat, avārum;
       et ___s quī captat qu__, Mariān_, velit.
      Tū t__en hu__ tabulīs h____dem, stulte, suprēmīs
       s____is et esse t__ vīs, furiōse, l____.
    5 "Mūnera m____ t__en mīsit." Sed ____t in hāmō.
      Et pisc_____ pisc__ amāre p_____?
      ___cine dē___bit vērō tua f___ dolōre?
       Sī c_____ ut plōret, __s, Mariāne, ____l.
                                            Martial

R20 Oculō Philaen__ s____r alterō __ōrat.
      Quō f___ istud quaeri___ ____? Lusca est.
                                            Martial

Third removal: unit 7

R21 Dēclāmās ____ē, causās ag___, Attice, ____ē;
       historiās _____ās, carmina _____a fa____;
       compōnis ____ē mīmōs, epi_____ata ____ē;
       ____us gr_____icus, ____us es astrologus;
    5 et bellē ca___s et s_____s, A_____, bellē;
       bellus es ____e lyr___; bellus es ____e pilae.
       Nīl b____ cum f_____, f_____ tamen omnia bellē.
       V__ d___m quid sīs? Magnus __ ardaliō.
                                                    Martial

UNIT 7

R22 ___ v_____ ___ ūvā

       F___ ___ācta vulpēs altā in v_____
       ūvam appetē_____, s____īs sal_____ vīribus.
       _____ tangere ut nōn potuit, ____cēdēns ___t,
       "____dum mātūra es; n___o acerbam s___ere."
    5 ____, facere quae ____ possunt, _____īs ēlevant,
       āscrībere hoc d___bunt ex_____ ___ibī.
                                                    Phaedrus

R23 _ē v_____s ho_____

       Pērās i___osuit J_____ nōbīs ____ās:
       propriīs ___plētam vitiīs _____ tergum d___it;
       aliēnīs _____ pectus suspend___ grav___.

       H__ r_ vidēre nostra m_____ nōn possumus;
    5 __iī ____l d_____unt, cēnsōrēs sumus.
                                                    Phaedrus

R24 V_____ ad p_____ tr_____

       Persōnam _____ f___e vulpēs vīd_____.
       "Ō ___anta ___ciēs" inquit "cerebrum nōn h___et!"
       Hoc illīs d___um est quibus h_____m et gl___am
       Fortūna _____uit, sēnsum com_____ abs___it.
                                                    Phaedrus

R25 _____er ad l_____ c_____iātor

Sibi __n cavēre et _____īs cōnsil____ dare
st____um es___ paucīs os_____āmus versibus.

____pressum ab aquilā, flētūs et dant___ ____avēs,
leporem objūrgā____ passer. "U___ p___nīcitās
5 nōta" inquit "illa est? Q___d ita cessā'_____ ped___?"
Dum ____quitur, i____um accipiter n_____pīnum rapit
ques___que vān___ clā____antem interficit.
Lepus sēmiani_____: "Mortis ē__ s____cium!
Quī m_____ sē_____us nostra ir____ēbās mala,
10 s_____ī que___lā fāta dēplōrās t___."
Phaedrus

UNIT 8

R26 C_____ per fl____um carnem f___ēns

Āmittit meritō pr____ium quī al____um ap____it.

Canis per _____men c_____m cum f_____t natāns,
lymphārum in spec_____ v___it si____lācrum suum,
aliamque praed___ ab alterō f___rī put_____,
5 ēripere vo____it. V____um dēcepta av____tās,
et ____em t_____bat ō___ dīmīsit cibum,
n____ ____em petēbat ad____ potuit tangere.
Phaedrus

Third removal: unit 9

R27 M___ du_ et l___ōnēs

    Mūlī grav___ sarcinīs _bant d__;
    ūn__ f__ēbat fi__ōs cum pecūniā,
    alter t__entēs multō s___ōs hord__.
    Ill_ onere dīv__ celsā cervīce ē___et
5 cl__umque collō jact__ t___innābulum;
    c__es quiētō sequitur __ placidō gr___.
    S___tō l___ēs ex īn__iīs advolant;
    dīrip___ n__mōs; neglegunt vī_ hordeum;
    interque c__dem ferr_ mūlum s__ciant.
10 Sp__iātus igi__ cāsūs c__ flēret suōs,
    "Equ___" in___ alter "m_ contemptum gaudeō;
    __m n__il āmīsī nec sum l__sus vulnere."

    Hōc argū___tō tū__ est hominum te__itās;
    magnae perī_'__ __nt opēs ob__xiae.
                                 Phaedrus

UNIT 9

S32 Bona opīn__ h___um tūtior pec___ est. *Publilius Syrus*
S33 V__ius arg___um est aurō, vir___bus aurum. *Horace*
S34 Ta__ō __jor fāmae siti_ est quam virtūtis! *Juvenal*
S35 Intolerā___ius nihil est __am f___a dīves. *Juvenal*
S36 __id clā___ ast___? *Motto*
S37 Sīmia qu__ similis turpissima bēs___ __bīs! *Ennius*
S38 Multō grā___ venit qu__ facilī quam quod plēnā ma__ datur. *Seneca*

R28 R__ r___a et b__

    In__s, potentem d__ vult im__ārī, perit.

    __ prātō quon__m rāna cōnspexit b___m,
    et t__ta invidiā t___ae ma___ūdinis
    rūgōsam īnflāvit pe__em. T__ nāt__ suōs
5 interrogāvit an b__e esse_ lāt___.
    I__ negā'runt. R__us intendit c__em
    ma___ nī__, et similī quaesīvit m___
    qu__ major esset. I___ dīx__nt bovem.
    Novi___mē __dignāta, dum vult v__dius
10 īnflāre s___, ruptō j__uit c__ore.
                                 Phaedrus

R29 Ad l__idem Torquāt__ habet praetōria qu____um;
    ad quār____, br____ rūs __mit Otācilius.
    Torquātus nitidās v__iō dē m__more th__mās
    exstr__it; cucum__ f____t Otācilius.
 5 Dis__uit dāphn____ suō Torquāt__ in agrō;
    cast__eās centum s__it O_____.
    Cōns____ Torqu____, vīcī fuit il__ magister;
    nōn ____nor in tantō v__us h__ōre sibī.
    Grand__ __t exiguam b__rānam rūperat ōl__,
10 s__, puto, T_____s rumpet O_____m.
                                    Martial

R30 O__ēs aut v__ulās h__ēs amīcās
    a__t t__pēs v__līsque foediōrēs.
    Hās dūcis comi____ trahis____ __cum
    per c__vīvia, portic__, th_____.
 5 S__ formō____, Fabulla, s__ puella es.
                                    Martial

R31 P__it Gemel____ __ptiās Marōnillae
    et cupit __ īnstat __ precātur et dō____.
    Ad__ne pulch__ est? __mmō, foedius nīl est.
    Quid erg__ in il__ p____tur et placet? Tussit.
                                    Martial

R32 Septima __am, Philerōs, tibi con__tur u____ in agrō.
    Pl__ nūll__, Philerōs, quam t____ reddit ager.
                                    Martial

R33 Sunt bo__, sunt qu__dam mediocria, sunt mala pl____
    __ae legis __c. Aliter nōn fit, Avīt__, liber.
                                    Martial

R34 C__ta suō gladium c__ trād_____ Arria Paetō
    __em dē ____ceribus strīnx____t ipsa suīs,
    (sī qua f__ēs) "Vulnus quod fēcī nōn dolet," in____
    "s__ tū quod f__iēs, h__ mihi, Paete, dolet."
                                    Martial

UNIT 10

S39 Fr_____r, __n fl_____r. *Motto*
S40 Tra_____ omn__ st____ō laudis. *Cicero*

Third removal: unit 10

S41 V__eō m__ōra probōque, dē__iōra sequor. *Ovid*
S42 Prō__dimur qu_ dūcit qu__que voluntās. *Lucretius*
S43 N__entēs morimur, fīn__que a_ orīgine pendet. *Manilius*
S44 Tempora m__ntur, nōs _t mūtāmur in ill__. *Borbonius(?)*

R35 R_____ _____ quīdam, cār__sime Jūlī,
    qu__ mē Rōma legit; r_____ _____.
  Rumpitur invidiā _____ tur__ semper in om__
    mōnstrāmur dig____; r_____ _____.
5 Rumpitur _____ tr__uit quod Caesar uter____
    __s __hi n__rum; rumpitur invidiā.
  Rumpitur invidiā quod __s mi_ d__ce sub urbe est
    p__aque in urbe domus; _____ _____.
  Rumpitur invidiā _____ sum __cundus ____cīs,
10   quod convī__ frequēns; _____ _____.
  Rumpitur invidiā _____ a__mur quodque pr__āmur.
    R_____ qu__uis rumpitur _____.
                         Martial

R36 Quod fro____ Selium nūbilā vid__, Rūf_,
  quod ambul____r porticum ter__ sē__,
  lūgubre qui__am quod ta__t piger vult__,
  quod p__e terram nāsus in____ēns ta__it,
5 quod dex____ p__tus pulsat et c__am vellit_
  nōn ille amīcī fāta l__get a__ fr__is;
  u_____e nātus vīvit et pr__or __at;
  salva __t et ux__ sarcinaeque servī____;
  nihil __lōnus __licusque dēcox__.
10 Maer__is ig____ causa q__? Domī cēnat.
                         Martial

R37 Mīrā__ __terēs, Vacerra, s__ōs
  __c laud__ nisi m__uōs poētās.
  Īgnōsc__ p__imus, Vacerra: t_____
  nōn e__, ut pl__am __bī, perīre.
                         Martial

R38 Nōn dōn__ tibi cūr me__ l____lōs
  ō__tū totiēns __ exi__tī
  m__ris, Theodōre? __na __sa est:
  dōn__ tū m____ __ tuōs libellōs.
                         Martial

R39 Scrīb____ m__ quereris, Vēlōx, epigramm____ longa.
      Ipse n____l scrībis: t__ breviōra fac__.
                                                Martial

R40 N__ere vīs Prīscō. Nōn m__or, Paula; s__ī'stī.
      ____ere t__ nōn vult Prīsc__, et ille sapit.
                                                Martial

R41 Uxōrem ___n v__ Pollam, __c Polla marītum
      tē vult. Bunn__, sapis, __c __nus illa sapit.
                                      John Parkhurst,
                            Bishop of Norwich (1512-1575)

R42 Quod c__vīvāris sine mē tam s__pe, Luperc__.
      __vēnī n__eam quā ratiōne __ibī.
      Īrāscor. L____ ūs____ vocēs mittāsque rog__que —
      "Quid ____iēs?" inquis? Quid ____iam? ____iam.
                                                Martial

R43 T__ Sētīna quidem semper __l Massic__ pōnis,
      Pāpyl__, sed rūmor tam bona v____ n____t.
      Dīceris hāc factus cael____ qu____r es__ lagōnā.
      ____ putō ____ crēdō, Pāpyle, ____ sitiō.
                                                Martial

UNIT 11

S45 Au__, __dē, t__ē, sī vīs vīvere in pāce. *Medieval*
S46 B____ f__re magnam di__e fortūnam. *Horace*
S47 Sī __id ag__, prūdenter ag__ et respice fīnem. *Translation of Aesop*
S48 D____e e__ i____ā. *Anonymous*

R44 Ae____tās ūnō d____ēns aut s__ius annō;
      nec i____ s__ nōbīs hoc, Polycharme, n____t.
      Nam qu____ns surg__, sōtēria posc__ amīcōs.
      Sit pud__: aegr____ jam, Polycharme, s__el.
                                                Martial

Third removal: unit 12

R45 _ōn dē vī _eque caede _ec venēnō,
     s__ līs est m____ d_ tribus capellīs.
     Vī_nī queror hās _esse f__tō.
     Hoc j__ex sibi postul___ __obārī.
   5 Tū C____s Mithridāticum___ b__lum
     e_ p__jūria P__icī furōris
     __ Sullās Mariōs___ Mūciōs___
     m___ā vōce sonās manū___ tō__.
     Jam ___, Postume, __ tribus ca___īs.
                                          Martial

R46 _um mē c____rēs, mittē___ mūnera nōbīs.
     P___quam cēpistī, dās m___, Rūf_, nihil.
     Ut captum t__eās, captō quo___ mūn___ mitte,
     dē caveā f___at nē mal_ pāst__ aper.
                                          Martial

R47 L____ _t a____

     Ad r__um eu__em lupus et agnus v__erant
     s___ com___sī. Superior stā__t lupus,
     longē___ īnf__or agnus. ___c fauce improbā
     latrō in___ātus j__giī c__sam intulit.
   5 "Cūr" in___ "turb___ntam f__istī mihī
     aquam b___ntī?" L__iger contrā timē__:
     "___ possum, quae__, fac__ quod quereris, lupe?
     Ā __ dēcu__it ad __ōs haustūs liquor."
     Repul___ __le vēri__tis vīribus,
  10 "__ te hō_ sex mēnsēs male" __t "dīxistī mihī."
     Respondit ___us: "__idem nātus nōn __am."
     "Pater, Her___, tu__" ille inquit "male dīxit m___."
     Atque it_ c__reptum lacerat injūstā ne___.
     H__c propter illōs scr__ta est hominēs f__ula
  15 quī fictīs causīs innocentēs opprimunt.
                                          Phaedrus

UNIT 12

S49 Ē_ ego Fort___! Sī stārem s____ sub ūnā
     et nōn m___rer, numquam "F____" v___rer
                                          Medieval

S50 S__ __em b____ātum faceret sua barba beātum,
in mundī circ_ n__ esset s__ctior hircō.
Medieval

S51 __ foret in terrīs, r__ēret Dēmocrit__. *Horace*

R48 Nūbere _____ cupit nōbīs; ego d__ere Paul__
_ōlo: anus est. V____em, sī m__is esset anus.
Martial

R49 V_____ __ co__us

Quī sē laudārī g__det v__bīs s__dolīs,
f____ dat p__nās turpī paenite____.

Cum dē fenestrā c____s r____um c__eum
co__sse ve__et, celsā re____ēns arbore,
5 v____ēs invīdit; d__nde sīc coe__t loquī:
"Ō __ī tuārum, corve, p__nārum est n__or!
Quantum de__ris corpore et vu__ū g__is!
__ vōcem hab____, nūlla prior āles f____t!"
At ille st____us, d__ vult v__em ostendere,
10 lāt_ ōre ēmīs__ cāseum, quem ce____iter
dolōsa v____s avid__ rapuit d____ibus.
Tum dē____ ingemuit corvī dēcep____ st__or.
Phaedrus

R50 V____a, c__ella, o__s, et leō

Numquam est fidē____ cum p__ente s__ietās:
testātur h____ fābel__ prōposi____ meum.

____ca et ____ella et patiēns ovis injūr____
soc__ f__re cum l____e in saltibus.
5 Hī cum cēpiss____ cervum v__tī c__poris,
sīc est lo__tus, par_____ fac____, leō;
"E__ prīmam tollō, n____nor quon____ 'Leō.'
Secundam, qu__ _um fortis, tribuē____ mihī.
T__ quia p____ valeō, mē sequētur ter____.
10 Malō af____iētur, sī quis qu__tam t__igerit."
Sīc tōtam pr__dam sō__ improbitās abs____it.
Phaedrus

Third removal: unit 13

R51 V_____ _t c_____

    Homō in per__'lum s____l _c vēnit callidus,
    re____īre effug____ qu__rit alterius malō.

    _um dēcidis____ vulpēs in pu__um īnscia
    et a__iōre claudere____ m__gine,
5 dēvēn__ hir__s s__iēns in eundem locum.
    S____l rog__it esset _n dulcis liquor
    et cōpiō____, il__ fr__dem mōliēns:
    "Dēscende, amīc_! Tanta b__itās est ____ae
    vol__tās _t sati__ī nōn possit mea."
10 Im__sit s_ barbātus. Tum vulp____a
    ēvāsit p__eō, nī_ c__sīs cornibus,
    hircumque clau__ līquit haer____em vad__.
                                   Phaedrus

UNIT 13

S52 Mori_____ _ē salūtā____. *Based on Suetonius*

R52 A____ __ am_____

    Anus j__ēre ____dit ēpōtam amph____,
    ad____ Falernā faece ē te__ā n____lī
    o__rem quae j__ndum lātē sparge____.
    Hunc p__quam tōtīs a____a trāxit n__ibus:
5 "Ō suāvis ani__! __āle in tē d__am bonum
    anteh__ fu____, tālēs cum sint reliqu____?"

    Hoc ____ pertin____ dīcet quī mē n__erit.
                                   Phaedrus

R53 Īnscrīpsit t____līs s____em sc____rāta virōrum
    sē fēcisse Chlo__. Qu__ p____ simplicius?
                                   Martial

R54 Jact__ ____aequālem Matho mē fēcisse lib_____.
    S_ vērum est, laud__ c_____ nostra Mathō.
    ____ālēs scrīb__ l__rōs Calvīnus et Umber:
    aequ_____ l__er est, Crētice, q__ malus est.
                                   Martial

R55 **Lupus et v_____, jūd____ si____**

____cumque t__pī fraude se____ innōtuit,
eti__ sī vē____ dīcit, āmitt____ fidem.
Hocc __testātur br__is Aesōpī fābula.

L____s arguē____ v____m fūrtī crīmine;
5 n____bat illa sē es__ culpae pr____mam.
T____ jūdex inter illōs s__it sīmi____.
Ut____e causam _um perōrā'ss____ suam,
dīxis__ __rtur sīmius sentent____:
"Tū n__ vidē____ perdidisse qu__ petis;
10 t_ crēdō sur____uisse qu__ pulchrē negās."
Phaedrus

R56 **R_____ __ s_____**

V____nī fūris celebr__ v__it nūptiās
Ae____s et con_____ n__āre coepit:
"Uxōr__ qu____am Sōl cum __llet dūcere,
clām_____ rānae su__ulēre __ sīdera.
5 C__vīciō per__tus quaer__ Juppiter
caus____ querēlae. Qu_____m tu__ stāgnī incola
'Nu__' inquit 'omnēs ūn__ exūr__ lacūs
c__itque mi____ās ā__dā sēde ēmorī.
Qu____am fut_____ est, sī creā'rit līb_____?' "
Phaedrus

UNIT 14

S53 Vig___e ___ ___te. *Anonymous*

S54 Quaer___ Dominum, et ___et anima vestr_. *Anonymous*

S55 _um Fāta ___nunt, vīv___ laetī. *Seneca*

R57 ___la, ___ēs, et ___er

    Aquila in subl___ quercū n__um f___erat;
    fēl__ ca___nam nacta in med__ pepererat;
    sūs, nem___is cultrīx, f__um ad īm__ posuerat.
    T__ f___uitum f___s contubernium
5 fr__de et scelestā ___c ēv___it malitiā.
    Ad nīdum scandit v___cris. "Per___iēs" a__
    tibī p___ur, ___an et m___ae mihī!
    N__, f___re terram quod vid__ cottīdiē
    aprum īn___iōsum, quercum v__t ēv___ere,
10 ut n___ram in pl__ fac___ prōgeniem opprimat."
    T__rōre ___fūsō et perturbātīs s___ibus,
    dērēp__ a_ c__īle saetōsae suis.
    "M___ō" inquit "in p___'_ō sunt ___tī tuī.
    Nam, simul e__eris pāstum cum te___ō gre___,
15 a___ est parāta rap___ porcell__ tibī."
    Hunc qu___e tim___ postquam complēvit l___m,
    d__ōsa tū__ condidit sēsē ca___.
    ___de ēvag___ no__ū suspēnsō pede;
    _bi ēscā sē ___plēvit et prōlem su__,
20 pavōrem s___āns ___spicit tō__ diē.
    Ruīnam m___ēns a___la r__īs dēsidet;
    ap__ ra___nam vītāns nōn prōdit f___s.
    ___id m___a? Inediā sunt cōnsūmptī c__ suīs
    fēlīsque ca___līs lārgam pr___buērunt d__em.

25 Quantum h___ b___inguis saepe c__cinnet malī
    d___mentum habēre h___ stulta crēd___tās potest.
                                                 Phaedrus

R58   ___is ___ēlis

   Re_____ l____ālis stultīs gr__us est;
   vērum perītīs ir__tōs te__it d__ōs.

   Nocturnus c__ fūr p____m mīsisset ca__,
   objectō tem____ns an cibō pos____ c__ī,
 5 "__us!" ____t "linguam vīs meam prae____dere,
   __ l__rem pr_ rē dominī? Multum falleris.
   Namque is__ subita mē j____t benīgnī__
   v____lāre, faciās __ m__ culpā lucrum."
                                        Phaedrus

R59   N__ mihi d__ vīvus; dīcis post fāta d____rum.
         Sī __n es stultus, sc__, Maro, quid cu____.
                                        Martial

R60   Ā f____īs utcum____ spoliārī v_ _ōs
      (ament, a____tur) n__pe exemp____ discimus.

      Ae____is mediae quen____ mulier nōn r__is
      tenē____ (a__ōs c____ns ēlegantiā)
 5   a____ōsque e____dem pul____ juvenis cēperat.
      Am____, v__ērī dum volunt illī p__ēs,
      ca____lōs hominī l__ere coepēre __ vicem.
      Quī sē p__āret fingī cū__ m____rum
      c__vus r____te factus est. N__ funditus
10   c__ōs puella, n____ōs anus ēvell____t.
                                        Phaedrus

R61   Quod l__ā caput al____ās, Charīn_,
      n__ aur__ tibi sed dol____ capillī.
                                        Martial

UNIT 15

R62 S____ _ fr_____

Praeceptō m____tus s__pe tē cōns___erā.

Ha__bat quīdam fīl____ tur___simam
_demque in__gnem pulchrā faciē ____ium.
Hī spe__lum, in c___edrā _ātris ut positum fuit,
5 puerīliter lūdent__ f___e īnspexēr____.
Hic s_ f____ōsum j___tat; illa īrāscitur
nec glōria___is su__inet _ātris jocōs,
accipi____ (Quid __im?) c__cta in contumēliam.
Ergō ad patrem d__urrit laesū__ __ vicem
10 m___āque in___iā c__minātur fīlium.
v__ nātus qu__ rem fēminārum tetiger___.
Amplexus il__ utrumque et c__pēns _cula
dulcemque in a__ōs cāritāt__ partiē__:
"Cott__iē" inquit "sp_____ vōs ū__ volō;
15 tū f___am _ē corrumpās nēquitiae mal__;
tū f___em __ istam mōri____ vincās bonīs."
                                               Phaedrus

R63 ____us _d f____m

Laud__īs ūtili__a quae contempser__
s__pe invenīrī test__ haec n___ātiō est.

Ad f____ m cervus, cum b__isset, re_itit
et __ liquōre v__it effigiem s__m.
5 Ibi dum rāmōsa m__āns laud__ cornu_
crūrum____ nimi__ tenuitātem vi__perat,
vēnantum su__tō v__ibus conte___tus
per c__pum fugere c__pit et cursū l_ī
can__ ē__sit. Silva tum exc__it ferum,
10 in qu_ r__entīs impedī____ cornibus
lacerārī coep__ morsibus s__vīs can__.
Tunc moriēns ēdidis__ vōcem h__c dīci___:
"Ō m_ īnfēlīc__! Quī nun_ dēmum intellegō
ūtilia mihī _am f__rint quae d__pexeram
15 et quae laudā'__m, quantum lū__ūs hab__rint."
                                               Phaedrus

R64   L__ s____x, aper, t_____s, et asinus

Quīcum____ _mīsit dī__itātem prīstinam,
īgnāvīs ___iam joc___ est in cāsū gr____.

Dēf____us annīs et dēs__tus v__ibus
l__ cum jacēret sp____tum extrēm___ trahēns,
5   ap__ f__mineīs sp__āns vēnit dentibus
et vi____cāvit ictū ve____em inj____am.
Īnf____tīs taurus ___x c___fōdit cornibus
h____īle corpus. Asinus, __ vīdit fer___
___pūne l__dī, cal___bus frontem e___ūdit.
10 A__ ille ex____rāns: "Fortīs ___dīgnē tulī
mihi īns____āre; tē, nā___rae d___ecus,
___od ferre c___or, certē bis vide___ morī."
                                    Phaedrus

R65   ____us __ ___er

E____s s__āre solitus __ō fuerat sitim,
dum ___sē aper v____tat turbāvit vad___.
H____ o___a līs est. Sonipēs ī__tus ferō
auxilium petī'___ hominis. ___em do___ō levāns
5   red___t ad host___ laetus. Hunc tēlīs eq____
po_____am int___fēcit, sīc lo___tus trāditur:
"L___tor tulisse au____ium mē pr___ibus tuīs.
Nam praed___ cēpī et didicī qu___ s___ ūtilis."
Atque i__ co___it frēnōs i__ītum patī.
10 T__ maest___ ille: "Parvae vin____tam reī
dum qu___rō d___ēns, servitūtem re___erī."

___aec īrāc___dōs adm____bit fābula
im____e p___ius laedī quam dēdī alter___.
                                    Phaedrus

UNIT 16

S56   S__ t____issēs, philosophus mān____sēs. *Attributed to Boethius*
S57   Hectora qu___ ___'sset, sī fēl___ Troja fuisset? *Ovid*
S58   Ō f___ cāre, _____ nimis al___ volāre. *Medieval*
S59   ____ī _ē tan___e. *John*
S60   _____ barbam v___lere mortuō le____. *Martial*
S61   Cont__ ver____ōs nōlī contendere ver____. *Dionysius Cato*

Third removal: unit 16

R66   ____us et __ō vēnant__

  Virtū____ exp____, verbīs jact____s glōriam,
  īg____ōs fallit, n__īs est dēr____ī.

  Vēnārī, asel__ com____, cum vel____ leō,
  contēxit ____lum fr____ice et a____onuit simul
5 ut ____suētā ____ce terrēret fer____,
  fugientēs ipse exciper____. H__c au__tulus
  clāmōrem su____ō t____lit tōtīs v____bus
  ____vōque t____bat bestī____ mīrāculō.
  Quae, dum p____entēs exitūs nō____s p____unt,
10 leōnis aff____guntur horre____ im____ū.
  Quī, p____quam caede ____ssus est, asin____ ēvocat
  jubet____ vōcem pr____ere. Tunc i____ īnsolēns:
  "Quālis vidē____ o____ra tibī vōcis me____?"
  "Īnsīgnis" ____it "sīc __, nisi nō's____ tuum
15 animum g____sque, similī f____ssem me____."
                                    Phaedrus

R67 Quid D____ int____at, nōlī per____rere sorte;
  quid st____uat dē __, sine tē dēlīberat i____.
                                Dionysius Cato

R68 Mus____a __ ____ō

  M____tēla ab homine prēnsa, cum īn____ntem n__em
  ef____gere vel__t, "P__ce, quaesō," inquit "mihī,
  qu__ tibi molestīs mūribus pūr__ dom____."
  Resp____dit ille, "F____rēs __ī causā meā,
5 grātum e____et et d____issem v____iam supplicī.
  Nunc, qu__ lab____ās ut fruāris re____iīs
  quās sunt r____ūrī, simul et ips____ dēvor____,
  nōlī imp____re vānum b____ficium m____."
  Atque i__ locūtus im____bam lētō d__it.

10 Hoc in sē dict__ dēbent il__ āgnōsc____,
  quōrum prīvāta s____it ūtili____ s____,
  et mer____um in__e jactant ____prūdentibus.
                                    Phaedrus

R69 ___squis Flā___niam teris, v___tor,
 n___ nōbile praeterī___ m___mor.
 Urbis dē___ciae s___ēsque N___ī,
 ar___ ___ grātia, lūsus ___ voluptās,
5 Rōmānī d___us ___ d___or theātrī
 ___que omnēs V___erēs Cupīdinēs___
 hōc s___ con___ta quō Paris se___chrō.
                    Martial

R70 Cum ___a nōn ēdās, carpis ___a carmina, Lael___.
 C___pere vel nōlī ___stra vel ___e tua.
                    Martial

R71 Ūndeciēns ū___ surrēx'___, Zōile, c___,
 et m___āta tibi ___t synthesis ū_____s,
 s___or in___rēret madidā nē ves___ retentus
 et laxam te___is l___deret aura cut___.
5 Qu___ r___ ego nōn sūdō, quī tēc___, Zōile, cēnō?
 Frīgus enim mag___ s___thesis ūna f___t.
                    Martial

UNIT 17

S62 _____āgō ___enda ___t. *Cato (adapted)*
S63 Pānis f___ōrum nōn objici_____ c___ibus. *Matthew*
S64 Dēlī___andum est s___e, statuendum est s___l. *Publilius Syrus*
S65 D___ ap___andum est bellum, ut vincās celer___. *Publilius Syrus*
S66 Viti___ uxōris aut tollend___ aut ferend___ est. *Varro*

UNIT 18

S67 Dē_____andō d_____itur s___ientia. *Publilius Syrus*
S68 D_____erandō s___pe perit oc___iō. *Publilius Syrus*
S69 N___andī cau___ avārō numquam d___icit. *Publilius Syrus*
S70 L___endī semper oc_____ō est, ___iendī nōn semper. *Pliny the Younger*
S71 Breve . . . tempus ae___is; satis est longum ___ bene honestēque v___ndum. *Cicero*
S72 Jūstitia est cōnst___ et perpetua voluntās jūs ___m ___que tribuendī. *Justinian*
S73 Male im_____ndō su___um imperium āmi___itur. *Publilius Syrus*

Third removal: unit 21

R72 Nihil ... ___e r___ne f___um est. *Seneca*
R73 C___ scrībendō nōn fit ut bene scrībātur; b___ s___ fit ut citō. *Quintilian*
R74 Sapientia ... a___ vīve___ put___ est. *Cicero*
R75 Ratiōne, nōn ___, ___cenda ad___entia est. *Publilius Syrus*
R76 N___il ___endō hominēs male ___ere discunt. *Marcus Porcius Cato*

UNIT 19

S74 Nēmō est ___m fortis q___ rei novitāte per___tur. *Caesar*
S75 Nōn l___ in b___ bis pe___āre. *Anonymous*
S76 Semel in a___ō ___et īnsān___. *Anonymous*
S77 Qu___ licet J___ nōn licet b___. *Anonymous*
S78 Ē___e opo___ ut vīv___, nōn vīvere ut edās. *Anonymous*

UNIT 21

S79 Spectātum v___; veniunt spect___ ut ips___. *Ovid*

Question words

English equivalents are in italics. They are only approximations of the Latin meanings. Note that, wherever applicable, an appropriate pronoun may be used in place of the noun called for by a given question word.

An?
Asks a question with an implied alternative. (**An bonus est?** *Is he good (or not)?*)

Ā quibus?
a. *By whom?* Asks for a personal noun in the abl pl; usually used with a passive verb. (Abl sg: **Ā quō?**)
b. *From whom? From what places or things?* Asks for a personal or nonpersonal noun in the abl pl. (Abl sg: **Ā quō?**)

Ā quō?
a. *By whom?* Asks for a personal noun in the abl sg; usually used with a passive verb. (Abl pl: **Ā quibus?**)
b. *From whom? From what place or thing?* Asks for a personal or nonpersonal noun in the abl sg. (Abl pl: **Ā quibus?**)

Cui?
a. *To whom? For whom? For what?* Asks for a noun in the dat sg. (Dat pl: **Quibus?**)
b. *Whom? What?* When used with a verb that patterns with the dat, **Cui?** asks for the sg complement of the verb. (Dat pl: **Quibus?**)

Cujus?
Whose? Asks for a gen sg noun. (Gen pl: **Quōrum?**)

Cūr?
Why? Answered by a subordinate clause with **quod, quia,** or **cum**; or an abl; or **propter** or **ob** with the acc. See also **Quam ob rem?** and **Quā rē?**

Question words

-ne?
Asks a neutral question expecting either a yes or a no answer.

Nōnne?
Asks a question expecting a positive answer. (**Nōnne bonus est?** *He's good, isn't he?*)

Num?
Asks a question expecting a negative answer. (**Num bonus est?** *He's not good, is he?*)

Quā?
By what route? By what means? Asks for an abl sg noun. See also **Quō?**

Quā condiciōne? Quibus condiciōnibus?
Under what condition(s)? Answered by a **sī** clause.

Quae rēs?
What things? Asks for a nonpersonal noun in the nom pl. (Nom sg: **Quid?**)

Quālis-e?
What sort of? Asks for an adj of quality, such as **bonus**.

Quāliter?
How? Asks for an adverb, such as **cautē** or **fortiter**. Compare **Quō modō?**

Quam?
How? (As in **Quam diū?** *How long?*)

Quam ob rem?
For what reason? Why? Answered by a subordinate clause, or an abl, or **propter** or **ob** with the acc. See also **Cūr?** and **Quā rē?**

Quandō?
When? Asks for a noun or noun phrase in the abl. See also **Quō tempore?**

Quantus-a-um?
How big? Asks for an adj of size, such as **magnus** or **minimus**.

Quā rē?
For what reason? Why? Answered by a subordinate clause, or an abl, or **propter** or **ob** with the acc. See also **Cūr?** and **Quam ob rem?**

Quās rēs?
What things? Asks for the acc pl of a nonpersonal noun. (Acc sg: **Quid?**)

Quem? Quam?
Whom? Asks for the acc sg of a personal noun. (Acc pl: **Quōs?**)

Quī? Quae?
Who? Asks for the nom pl of a personal noun. (Nom sg: **Quis?**)

Quī? Quae? Quod?
Which? What? Used in any case to elicit an adj in the corresponding case. (**Quās fēminās vīdistis?** *Which women did you see?*)

Quibus?
a. *To whom? For whom?* Asks for the dat pl of a personal noun. (Dat sg: **Cui?**)
b. *By what things?* Asks for the abl pl of a nonpersonal noun. (Abl sg: **Quō?**)

Quibus auxiliīs?
By what means? Asks for an abl pl noun. (Abl sg: **Quō auxiliō?**)

Quibuscum?
With whom? Asks for the abl pl of a personal noun, preceded by the preposition **cum**. (Abl sg: **Quōcum?**)

Quid?
What? Asks for a nonpersonal noun in the nom or acc sg. (Nom pl: **Quae rēs?** Acc pl: **Quās rēs?**)

Quid agendō?
By doing what? Asks for a gerund in the abl.

Quid agit? Quid ēgērunt? Quid agat?
What is he doing? What did they do? What should he do? and so forth, for the various persons and tenses of **agō**. Asks for a verb, frequently with its subject, and for the verb complement, if any.

Quid sīgnat? Quid sīgnificat?
What is the meaning of . . . ?

Quis?
Who? Asks for a personal noun in the nom sg. (Nom pl: **Quī?**)

Quō?
a. *By what means?* Asks for a nonpersonal noun in the abl. See also **Quā?** and **Quibus?**
b. *To what place?* (As in **Quō vādis?**) Asks for an acc noun with a preposition such as **ad** or **in**.
c. *Whom? What?* When used with a verb that patterns with the abl, **Quō?** asks for the verb complement.

Question words

Quō auxiliō?
By what aid? With what help? How? Answered by a noun in the abl sg. (Abl pl: **Quibus auxiliīs?**)

Quō cōnsiliō?
For what purpose? Answered by a purpose clause (with **ut** or **nē**) with the subjunctive.

Quōcum?
With whom? Asks for a personal noun in the abl sg, preceded by the preposition **cum**. (Abl pl: **Quibuscum?**)

Quō ex locō?
From what place? Answered by a prepositional phrase with **ex (ē)** or **ab (ā)** and an abl noun, such as **ex urbe**. See also **unde**.

Quō īnstrūmentō? Quō membrō? etc.
By what instrument? By what part of the body? and so forth. Asks for a nonpersonal noun in the abl sg.

Quō modō?
How? In what manner? Asks for a noun in the abl, usually within an expression such as **magnā laude** or **magnā cum laude**. Compare **Quāliter?**

Quōrum? Quārum?
Whose? Asks for a gen pl noun (Gen sg: **Cujus?**)

Quōs? Quās?
Whom? Asks for a personal noun in the acc pl. (Acc sg: **Quem?**)

Quot?
How many? Answered by count words, such as **quattuor** or **multī**.

Quō tempore?
At what time? When? Asks for a nonpersonal noun in the abl. See also **Quandō?**

Quotiēns?
How many times? Answered by words like **bis** or **saepe**.

Quotus-a-um?
What number? (in a series) Answered by ordinal numbers, such as **tertius**.

Ubī?
In what place? Where? Asks for a nonpersonal noun in the abl, preceded by a preposition such as **in** or **sub**. (**Ubī** means *when* only as a relative.)

Unde?
From what place? From what time? Asks for a nonpersonal noun in the abl, usually preceded by a preposition such as **ex** or **ab**. See also **Quō ex locō?**

Uter? Utra? Utrum?
Which? (of the two) May be answered by adjs such as **magnus, melior**, or **fortissimus**; or by a choice between two alternatives (as in **Uter dux Galliam vīcit, Caesar an Vercingetorīx?**).

Utrum . . . an?
Asks for a choice between two items: *Is it this or that?*

Index to subjects

Boldface numerals in parentheses indicate Unit numbers in the programmed text for Level Two. Numerals in regular type indicate page numbers in this Reference Notebook.

Abbreviations, 1
Ablative absolute **(9, 12)**, 50
   in dates **(2, 16)**
Ablative case, uses of **(9)**,
     46-50, 103
   in ablative absolute, 50
   to modify adjective, 49
   to modify comparatives **(9)**,
     49-50
   to modify noun, 48
   to modify passive verb, 46
   to modify verb, 46-48
   as verb complement **(16, 18)**,
     50
Accusative case, uses of, 45-46
   as direct object, 45
   as exclamatory accusative **(15)**,
     46
   to modify adjective, 46
   to modify noun, 46
   to modify verb **(9, 20, 24)**,
     45-46
Active voice
   paradigms of
     imperfective, 17-19
     perfective, 21-22
   syntax of, 64-66
ad: *see also* Prepositions
   with gerund to express
     purpose, 79, 89
   with gerundive to express
     purpose, **(17)**, 77, 89
Adjectivals
   list of, 35
   syntax of, 85

Adjectives, 6-10, 54-59; *see also*
   Pronouns; Demonstrative
   pronouns and adjectives;
   Determinative pronoun and
   adjective; Indefinite pronouns
   and adjectives; Intensifying
   pronoun and adjective;
   Interrogative pronoun and
   adjective
Adjectives, morphology of, 6-10
   comparison of **(9)**, 8-9
     irregular, 8
     regular, 8
   gender of, 6
   paradigms of
     first and second declension,
       7
     special, declension of, 9
     third declension, 7, 97
Adjectives, syntax of, 54-59
   gender of, 56-59
   with genitive **(12, 16, 18)**
   inflection of, 56
   order of, in sentence, 87
   in superlative, 40, 53
Adverbial numerals, 34, 38, 84
Adverbs
   comparison of **(9)**, 35, 55
   formation of, 34
   syntax of, 84
alius (special adjective), 10
alter (special adjective), 10
Apposition, 40
Aspect, verb inflection for, 75
   English-Latin contrasts in,
     104-105

   forms of; *see* Tense-Aspect-
     Mood
   imperfective, 75
   perfective, 75
Assimilation **(5, 7, 14)**, 95

Basic Text (Level Two), 109-129
bonus, comparison of **(10)**, 8

Cardinal numerals, 35-37, 87
Case, noun; *see* Noun cases:
   Ablative; Accusative;
   Dative; Genitive;
   Locative; Nominative;
   Vocative
causā with gerund or gerundive
   to express purpose, 90
Characteristic vowel, of nouns
   meaning of, 2
   of first declension, 3
   of second declension, 3
   of third declension, 4
   of fourth declension, 5
   of fifth declension, 5
Characteristic vowel, of verbs
   of four conjugations, 14
   meaning of, 14, 98
Clozes
   introduction to, 107-108
   first removal, 130-149
   second removal, 150-172
   third removal, 173-193

continued

Commands, 67, 91-93; *see also*
    Imperative mood
  direct, 92-93
  indirect, 91
  negative, 93
Comparative form
  of adjectives (9), 8-9
  of adverbs (9), 35
Comparison
  of adjectives (9), 8-9
  of adverbs (9), 35, 55
Complement of verb; *see* Verb
    complement
Conjunctions; *see* Coordinating
    conjunctions; Subordinating
    conjunctions
Connectors, sentence, 30, 81
Coordinating conjunctions
  list of, 30
  syntax of, 79-80
cum
  with indicative, 68, 80-81
  with subjunctive (6), 68, 80-81

Dates, Roman system of (2, 20)
  ablative absolute in (2, 16), 50
  days of the month in (20),
    102-103
Dative case, uses of, 50-52
  with adjectives, 51
  with compound verbs (18), 51
  in dedicatory inscriptions, 52
  in double dative (16), 52
  to indicate agent, 51
  as indirect object, 51
  as verb complement (16),
    50-51
Declensions, noun; *see* Noun
    declensions
Defective nouns, 3, 95-96
Definition, progressive, 40
Demonstrative pronouns and
    adjectives (2)
  declensions of, 12-13
  syntax of, 60-61, 87
Deponent verbs (1, 3, 10), 26, 65
  semi-deponent verbs (2), 66
Determinative pronoun and
    adjective (idem)
  declension of, 12
  syntax of, 60
Direct command, 92-93
Distributive numerals (23), 37
Double dative (16), 52

dum
  with indicative, 70
  with subjunctive (20), 70
duo, declension of, 36

egō, nōs
  declension of, 10
  syntax of, 59
Embedded elements (22)
Ending
  on nouns, 2
  on verbs, 14
English-Latin contrasts
  of aspect in verbs, 104-105
  of number in nouns, 100-101
Environment (in syntax), 39
eō, conjugation of, 27-29
Exclamatory accusative (15), 46

facile, as adverb, 54
Factitive verbs, 45, 102
ferō, conjugation of, 27-30
fīō, conjugation of, 27-29
First imperative
  forms, 19
  use, 67, 92
Forms, verb #1-#11; *see*
    Tense-Aspect-Mood
Future active participle (13), 15,
    24, 76, 91; *see also* Participles
Future passive participle; *see*
    Gerundive; Participles

Gender, 56
  of adjectives, 6, 56-59
  in nouns, 3-5, 56-58
Genitive case, uses of (18), 52-53
  to modify adjectives (12,16,18)
    53
  to modify nouns, 53, 103
  as verb complement (22), 52-53
Gerund (18)
  contrast with gerundive (18)
  to express purpose, 89-90
  forms of, 25
  uses of, 79
Gerundive (future passive
    participle) (17)
  contrast with gerund (18)
  with dative agent, 51
  to express purpose (17), 89-90
  forms of (17), 25
  syntax of, 76-77
Greek accusative, syntax of, 46
Greek noun forms, 96-97

hic (2)
  declension of, 12
  syntax of, 60
Historical infinitive (23), 77

idem
  declension of, 12
  syntax of, 60
ille (2)
  declension of, 12
  syntax of, 61
Imperative mood (11, 14, 16)
  first imperative forms, 19
  second imperative forms, 100
  syntax of, 64, 67, 92
Imperfective aspect, 17-20, 75
  infinitives, 24
  meaning of, 75
  participles, 24
  stem of, 25
Impersonal passive (24), 65, 100
Impersonal verbs (19), 63, 68, 77
impūne, as adverb, 54
Indefinite pronouns and
    adjectives, 13-14
Indicative mood
  forms of: *see* Tenses #1-#6
  syntax of, 66-67
Indirect discourse (2, 6), 90-92
  indirect commands, 91-92
  indirect question (6), 68, 91
  indirect statement (2), 71, 90
  problems in reading (22)
Indirect object, 51
Indirect question (6), 91
  subjunctive in (15), 68
Indirect statement (2), 90
  infinitive in, 78
  subjunctive in, 71
Infinitive, historical (23), 77
Infinitives
  forms of, 24
  uses of (18, 21), 77-78,
    90-91, 101-102
Intensifiers
  list of, 31
  syntax of, 82
  word order of, 88
Intensifying pronoun and
    adjective (ipse)
  declension of, 12
  syntax of, 60
Interjections
  list of, 30
  syntax of, 82

Index

Interrogative adjective
  (quī), 13, 61-62
Interrogative pronoun and
  adjective (quis)
  declension of, 13
  syntax of, 62-63
Interrogators
  list of, 31
  syntax of, 82
Intransitive verbs, 64-65, 99-100
ipse
  declension of, 12
  syntax of, 60
Irregular verbs, conjugations of,
  27-29
is (14)
  declension of, 11
  syntax of, 59
iste (2)
  declension of, 12
  syntax of, 61

Latin prose
  connecting devices in (17)
  expression of direct command
    in, 92-93
  expression of purpose in,
    89-90
  indirect discourse in, 90-92
  involved sentence in (22)
  word order in, 86-88
Left-branching modifiers (22)
Leveling, 40
licet, as impersonal verb, 63
licet, as subordinating
  conjunction, 69
Locative case (10)
  form of, 95, 101
  use of, 54, 101

magis, to show comparative
  degree, 8, 35
magnus, comparison of, 8
mālō, conjugation of, 27-29
malus, comparison of, 8
maximē, to show superlative
  degree, 8, 35
Modifiers, right- and
  left-branching (22)
Mood, verb inflection for (4),
  66-71
  forms of; see Tense-Mood-
    Aspect
  imperative, 67
  indicative, 66-67
  subjunctive, see also
    Subjunctive mood
Morphology, explained, 2
multī, comparison of, 8
Multiplicative numerals, 38
multum, as adverb, 55
multus, comparison of, 8

Names, Roman (21)
Narrative tenses (19), 73, 105
nē, uses of (4, 5), 67-69, 89, 93
Necessity, expression of, 76
Negative command (16), 93
Negators
  list of, 31
  syntax of, 82
  word order of, 88
neuter (special adjective), 10
nōlō
  conjugation of, 27-29
  in negative commands, 93
Nominative case, uses of, 44
  in citation, 44
  as complement of connecting
    verb, 44
  as presentative nominative, 44
  as subject of verb, 44
  as vocative, 44
nōn, use of, in subjunctive (4), 68
Noninflected words
  classes of, 30-35
  syntax of, 79-85
Nonpersonal pronouns
  paradigms of, 11-13
  syntax of, 59-63
Noun, morphology of, 2-6
  cases of, 2
  characteristic vowel of, 3-5
  declensions of, 3-6; see also
    Noun declensions
  ending of, 2
  stem of, 2
Noun cases,
  morphology of, 2-6
  syntax of, 43-54
    ablative, 46-50; see also
      Ablative case
    accusative, 45-46; see also
      Accusative case
    dative, 50-52; see also
      Dative case
    genitive, 52-53; see also
      Genitive case
    locative, 54, 95; see also
      Locative case
    nominative, 44; see also
      Nominative case
    vocative, 53, 101; see also
      Vocative case
Noun declensions
  characteristic vowels of, 3-5
  comparative table of, 6
  gender of, 3-5, 56-58
  major, 3-5
  minor, 5
  paradigms of
    first, 3
    second, 3
    third, 4
    fourth, 5
    fifth, 5
Noun forms, Greek, 96-97
Noun inflection, 42-43
  for case, 43
  for number, 43
Noun substitutors
  defined, 32, 100
  list of, 32-34
  syntax of, 84
Nouns, defective, 3
Nouns of value, 52
nūllus (special adjective), 10
num (22)
Number, inflection for,
  in adjectives, 56
  English-Latin contrasts in,
    100-101
  in nouns, 43
  in pronouns, 60-61
  in verbs, 64
Numerals
  adverbial, 34, 38, 84
  cardinal, 35-37, 87
  declensions of unus, duo,
    trēs, 36
  distributive (23), 37
  multiplicative, 38
  ordinal, 35-37
  Roman, 36-37

Object of verb
  direct, 45
  indirect, 51
Omission of items, 41-43
Ordinal numerals, 35-37

continued

Participles (17)
  future active (13), 15, 24, 76, 91
  future passive (gerundive), 24, 76-77; *see also* Gerundive
  imperfective active ("present"), 24, 76
    declension of, 8
  perfective passive ("past"), 15, 24, 76
  syntax of, 76-77, 91
parvus, comparison of, 8
Passive voice
  paradigms of, 19-20, 22-23
    imperfective, 19-20
    perfective, 22-23
  syntax of, 64-65
"Past" participle, 15, 24, 76; *see also* Participles
pelagus, declension of, 96
Perfective active stem formation, 99
Perfective aspect, 21-25, 75
  infinitive, 24
  meaning of, 75
  participle, 24-25
  stem of, 21
Person verb, inflection for, 63-64
Personal pronouns
  order of, 88
  paradigms of, 10-11
  syntax of, 59
Poetic analysis, introduction to (2)
Poetical devices (2, 5, 6, 9, 10)
possum, conjugation of, 27-29
Prepositions
  list of, 31-32
  syntax of, 83
"Present" participle, 24, 76; *see also* Participles,
  declension of, 8
primum, as adverb, 54
Principal parts of verbs, 15
Progressive definition, 40
Pronouns, morphology of, 10-14
  demonstrative (2), 12-13
  determinative, 12
  indefinite, 13-14
  intensifying, 12
  interrogative, 13
  nonpersonal, 11-13, 59-63
  personal, 10-11
  reflexive, 11
  relative, 13

Pronouns, syntax of, 59-63, 88
Prose; *see* Latin prose
Purpose, expression of, 69, 89-90

Qualifiers
  list of, 32
  syntax of, 84
  word order of, 88
quam
  with comparative (9)
  as qualifier (9)
Question words
  in indirect question, 91
  list of, 194-198
qui (7)
  declension of, 13
  syntax of, 61-62
quid, as adverb, 54; *see also* quis
quin
  as sentence connector (23)
  with subjunctive (19), 69
quis
  declension of, 13
  as substitute for aliquis in *si* clauses, 13
  syntax of, 62-63
quod, as subordinating conjunction, 55

Reading Latin
  difficulties in (10, 12, 13)
  techniques of (14)
rēctum, as adverb, 54
Reflexive pronouns
  paradigm of, 11
  syntax of, 59
Relative pronoun (quī)
  declension of, 13
  syntax of, 61-62
Right-branching modifiers (22)
Roman names (21)
Roman numerals, 36-37

sē, declension of (1), 11
Second imperative, 92, 100
Semideponent verbs (2), 66
Sentence connectors
  list of, 30
  syntax of, 80-81
Sentence construction, 86-93
  expression of command in, 92-93
  expression of purpose in, 89-90
  indirect discourse in, 90-92
  word order in, 86-88

Sequence of tenses, 72-74
Slot (in syntax), 39
sōlus (special adjective), 10
Special adjectives, 10
Stem
  of nouns, 2
  of verbs; *see* Verb stems
Subject, 44
Subjunctive mood (4, 15), 67-71
  in direct commands, 92, 93
  in indirect discourse, 70, 91
  in main clauses, 67-68
  rules for tense in, 71-74
  in subordinate clauses, 68-71
  in tenses #7-#10; *see* Tense
Subjunctive of characteristic (13, 15), 71, 104
Subordinating conjunctions
  list of, 30
  order of, in clause, 81, 87
  syntax of, 80-81
sum
  conjugation of, 27-29
  with gerundive, 76
Superlative form
  of adjectives, 8, 40, 53
  of adverbs, 35
Supine (14, 19, 21)
  to express purpose, 90
  forms of, 25
  uses of, 46, 79
Syntax, explained, 39

Tense, verb inflection for, 71-75
  agreement of, in narrative, 72-73
  chart of, 74
  in indirect statement, 90-91
  sequence of tenses, 72
Tense-Aspect-Mood #1 (past imperfective indicative)
  active paradigm, 17
  passive paradigm, 19
  personal endings, 14
Tense-Aspect-Mood #2 (present imperfective indicative)
  active paradigm, 18
  as narrative tense (19), 73, 105
  passive paradigm, 19
  personal endings, 14
Tense-Aspect-Mood #3 (future imperfective indicative)
  active paradigm, 18
  in direct commands, 92
  passive paradigm, 19
  personal endings, 14

Index

Tense-Aspect-Mood #4 (past perfective indicative)
  active paradigm, 21
  passive paradigm, 22
  personal endings, 14
Tense-Aspect-Mood #5 (present perfective indicative)
  active paradigm, 21
  as narrative tense, 73, 105
  passive paradigm, 23
  personal endings, 14
Tense-Aspect-Mood #6 (future perfective indicative)
  active paradigm, 21
  passive paradigm, 23
  personal endings, 14
  use of, 105
Tense-Aspect-Mood #7 (past imperfective subjunctive) **(8, 12)**
  active paradigm, 18
  passive paradigm, 20
  personal endings, 14
  use of, 68, 72-74
Tense-Aspect-Mood #8 (present imperfective subjunctive) **(4, 5)**
  active paradigm, 18
  passive paradigm, 20
  personal endings, 14
  use of, 67, 72-74
Tense-Aspect-Mood #9 (past perfective subjunctive) **(12, 16)**
  active paradigm, 22
  passive paradigm, 23
  personal endings, 14
  use of, 68, 72-74
Tense-Aspect-Mood #10 (present perfective subjunctive) **(15)**
  active paradigm, 22
  passive paradigm, 23
  personal endings, 14
  use of, 72-74, 93
Tense-Aspect-Mood #11; *see* Imperative mood
tōtus, declension of, 9
Transitival verbs, 64
Transitive verbs, 64-65, 100
trēs, declension of, 36
tū, vōs
  declension of, 10
  syntax of, 59
tussis, declension of, 96

ūllus (special adjective), 10
ūnus
  declension of, 36
  special adjective, 10
ut
  uses of, 68-69, 89
  in purpose clauses **(5)**, 69, 89
  in result clauses **(12)**, 68
uter (special adjective), 10
uterque (special adjective) **(10)**, 10
utinam, use of **(4)**, 67
utrum, as interrogator, 55

Variant constructions, 40-43
Variant nouns
  of second declension, 96
  of third declension, 96
Verb, inflectional categories of
  aspect, 75
  mood, 66-71
  number, 64
  person, 63-64
  tense, 71-75
  voice, 64-66
Verb complement, 44
  in ablative case, 50
  in accusative case, 45
  in dative case, 50
  in genitive case, 52
  in nominative case, 44
  review of **(22)**
Verb conjugations, 16-29
  characteristic vowels of, 14
  irregular, 27-29
  paradigms of, 17-29
    index to, 16-17
  personal endings of, 14
  principal parts of, 15
Verb forms #1-#11; *see* Tense-Aspect-Mood
Verb participles; *see* Participles
Verb stems
  imperfective, 15, 17
  imperfective deponent, 26
  lexical, 14
  perfective active, 15, 21
    formation of, 99
  perfective passive, 15
Verbal nouns **(21)**; *see* Gerund; Infinitives; Supine
Verbs
  deponent **(1, 3, 10)**, 26, 65
  factitive, 45, 102
  intransitive, 64-65
  irregular, 27-29
  semideponent **(2)**, 66
  transitival, 64
  transitive, 64-65, 100
Verbs, morphology of
  characteristic vowels, 14, 98
  conjugations, 16-29; *see also* Verb conjugations
  endings, 14
  infinitives; *see* Infinitives
  overview chart of, 16
  participles; *see* Participles
  principal parts, 15
  stems; *see* Verb stems
Verbs, syntax of, 63-75
Verbs with two complements
  acc and acc, 45, 102
  acc and dat, 51
Verbum sentiendi (2), 45, 90-91
vērum, as sentence connector, 55, 81
Vocative case **(11)**, 53, 101
  form of, 2, 4
  use of, 53, 101
Voice, verb inflection for, 64-66; *see also* Active voice; Passive voice
volō, conjugation of, 27-29
Vowel, characteristic; *see* Characteristic vowel
Vowel changes, regular, 94-95
Vowel length, rules for **(1)**
Vowel shortening **(1, 4)**, 94-95
Vowel weakening **(1, 5, 7, 14)**, 94
vulgus, declension of, 96

Word formation **(14)**; *see also* Assimilation; Vowel shortening; Vowel weakening
Word order, 86-88

Latin Grammar & Resources

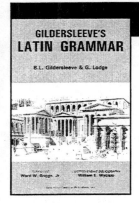

Gildersleeve's Latin Grammar
B.L. Gildersleeve & G. Lodge

The classic Latin grammar favored by many students and teachers with two new addtions:
+ Foreword by **Ward W. Briggs, Jr.**
+ Comprehensive bibliography by **William E. Wycislo**.

"Rightly interpreted, grammar is the culmination of philological study, and not its rudiment ... No study of literature can yield its highest result without the close study of language, and consequently the close study of grammar."

Basil L. Gildersleeve, *Selected Classical Papers*

"Compare his work with any other treatise hitherto in use, and its superiority will be manifest."

Southern Review

613 pp. (1895, third ed., reprint with additions 1997) paperback, ISBN 0-86516-353-7

New Latin Grammar
Charles E. Bennett

New Latin Grammar uses specific examples from primary sources to help students learn the inflections, syntax, sounds, accents, particles and word formations of the Latin language. It also includes a history of the Indo-European family of languages, the stages of the development of the Latin language and sections on prosody, the Roman calendar, Roman names, and definition and examples of figures of syntax and rhetoric.

xvi + 287 pp. (1908, Reprint 1995) paperback, ISBN 0-86516-261-1

New Latin Syntax
E. C. Woodcock

This book gives a historical account of the chief Latin constructions, aiming to equip students to interpret texts as well as to write correct Latin. The index of passages quoted makes it useful as a reference work for teachers. This is a necessary reference and an indispensable vademecum for teachers and advanced students.

xxiv + 267 pp. (1959, Reprint 1987) Paperback, ISBN 0-86516-126-7

A Handbook of Latin Literature
From the earliest times to the death of St. Augustine
H. G. Rose

This reference work offers a matchless overview of Latin literature. Also included is a supplementary bibliography by E. Courtney.

582 pp. (1936, rpt. 1996), Paperback, ISBN: 0-86516-317-0

Graphic Latin Grammar
James P. Humphreys

Four double-sided pages containing all your Latin grammar charts on sturdy card stock ready for insertion in a 3-ring notebook.

(1961, Reprint 1995) Four 3-hole-punched laminated reference cards, ISBN 0-86516-111-1

Elementary Latin Translation: Latin Readings for Review
A. E. Hillard and C. G. Botting, eds., with additions by Donald H. Hoffman

This graded reader is an excellent supplement to first-year Latin texts or as a review tool. The Latin is pure, simple, idiomatic, and easily understood by beginning students. Each review features two readings that acquaint the student with the chief events of Roman history and stories from Greek mythology. Latin references eliminate the need to consult other grammars.

vii + 192 pp. (1961, Reprint 1997), Paperback, ISBN 0-86516-403-7

BOLCHAZY-CARDUCCI Publishers, Inc.
orders@bolchazy.com